RENEWABLE ENERGIES

Renewable energy normally refers to usable energy sources that are an alternative to fuel sources, but without the negatively evaluated consequences of the replaced fuels. Although energy issues have a long tradition in sociology and other social sciences, it may now be high time to conceptualize these in sociological terms as the lynchpin in our understanding of the way societies are set to develop in the twenty-first century.

This concise book focuses on sociological attempts at better framing contemporary theories of energy transformations and to deliver an accessible overview on the relationships between different types of renewable energy sources and their practical usages in modern societies. A strong focus is laid upon new forms of environmental governance and unavoidable knowledge gaps triggered by attempts to transform contemporary energy systems into renewable ones.

Critical topics include the challenge of transition from centralized to decentralized system structures, the integration of renewable energies into existing energy structures or the replacement of these, coping strategies to unforeseen risks and conflict issues, and sociocultural reservations to new technologies connected to renewable energies.

Matthias Gross is Professor of Environmental Sociology at Helmholtz Centre for Environmental Research, UFZ, Leipzig and, by joint appointment, the University of Jena, Germany. His recent research has focused on the evolution of alternative energy systems, the centrality of ignorance in engineering, and experimental practices in society. His most recent monograph is *Ignorance and Surprise: Science, Society, and Ecological Design* (MIT Press, 2010).

Rüdiger Mautz is Senior Research Scientist at the Sociological Research Institute of Göttingen (SOFI), Germany. His recent research has concentrated on energy system transitions and the social dynamics of renewable energies. His most recent book (together with A. Byzio and W. Rosenbaum) is *Auf dem Weg zur Energiewende: Die Stromproduktion aus erneuerbaren Energien in Deutschland* (Universitätsverlag Göttingen, 2008).

'The ongoing transition to renewable energy sources is much more than a substitution of fossil fuels by alternative energy carriers. The great merits of this book are that it sheds light on the interdependency of new forms of energy provision with profound changes in our societies and that it shows that social sciences are essential for understanding this challenge.'

Harald Rohracher,
Professor of Technology and Social Change,
Linköping University

KEY IDEAS

Series Editor: PETER HAMILTON

Designed to compliment the successful *Key Sociologists*, this series covers the main concepts, issues, debates, and controversies in sociology and the social sciences. The series aims to provide authoritative essays on central topics of social science, such as community, power, work, sexuality, inequality, benefits and ideology, class, family, etc. Books adopt a strong "individual" line as critical essays rather than literature surveys, offering lively and original treatments of their subject matter. The books will be useful to students and teachers of sociology, political science, economics, psychology, philosophy, and geography.

Citizenship
Keith Faulks

Class
Stephen Edgell

Community – second edition
Gerard Delanty

Consumption
Robert Bocock

Globalization – second edition
Malcolm Waters

Lifestyle
David Chaney

Mass Media
Pierre Sorlin

Moral Panics
Kenneth Thompson

Old Age
John Vincent

Postmodernity
Barry Smart

Racism – second edition
Robert Miles and Malcolm Brown

Risk
Deborah Lupton

Social Capital – second edition
John Field

Transgression
Chris Jenks

The Virtual
Rob Shields

Culture – second edition
Chris Jenks

Human Rights
Anthony Woodiwiss

Childhood – second edition
Chris Jenks

Cosmopolitanism
Robert Fine

Nihilism
Bulent Diken

RENEWABLE ENERGIES

Matthias Gross and Rüdiger Mautz

Routledge
Taylor & Francis Group

LONDON AND NEW YORK

First published 2015
by Routledge
2 Park Square, Milton Park, Abingdon, Oxfordshire OX14 4RN

and by Routledge
711 Third Avenue, New York, NY 10017

Routledge is an imprint of the Taylor and Francis Group, an informa business

First issued in paperback 2015

British Library Cataloguing in Publication Data
A catalogue record for this book is available from the British Library

Library of Congress Cataloging in Publication Data
Gross, Matthias, 1969-
   Renewable energies / by Matthias Gross and Rüdiger Mautz.
      pages cm
   1. Renewable energy sources. 2. Energy policy–Social aspects.
   I. Mautz, Rüdiger. II. Title.
   TJ808.G76 2014
   333.79'4–dc23   2014010328

ISBN 978-0-415-85861-8 (hbk)
ISBN 978-1-138-19451-9 (pbk)
ISBN 978-0-203-79802-7 (ebk)

Typeset in Garamond and Scala
by Sunrise Setting Ltd, Paignton, UK

Contents

ILLUSTRATIONS

FIGURES

TABLES

1

INTRODUCTION

THE NEXT GREAT
EXPERIMENT

Research and theory in sociology often focus on unexpected and sometimes paradoxical phenomena. As such, they are concerned with the way in which alternative societal structures and fundamentally new social processes come about. This has led some scholars to argue that the Western world is subject to epochal breaks that periodically mark its entry into a new kind of society (the information society, the knowledge society, the risk society, for example), one that departs fundamentally from previous political, ecological, technical, or cultural orders. Meanwhile, other scholars point to long-term evolutionary processes, situating the emergence of novel aspects of society within longer term processes associated with modernity. This tension between focusing either on radical shifts or on long-term accounts can be observed in particular in the context of debates around alternative energy sources and energy transitions in twenty-first-century societies. On the one hand, it seems to be generally accepted that energy transitions are inherently gradual, incremental processes that cannot be driven forward by the formulaic style of thinking reflected in targets, such as 20 percent of total electricity produced from renewable energy sources by 2020 and 50 percent by 2050 (see Podobnik 2006, Smil 2010). On the other hand, a number of prominent figures are now speaking of peak oil, peak coal, indeed peak everything, thereby heralding an epochal break that is argued to be either coming soon or already upon us – whether by political will or by necessity (see Heinberg 2007, Scheer 2012, Urry 2013). In order to understand these shifts (however they may be conceptualized), sociological analysis needs to focus its attention on both the regional and local levels of decentralized energy initiatives, as well as on nationally and globally anchored processes of energy utilization.

Whereas sociologists, anthropologists, economists, political science scholars, and historians (among many others) have taken an innovation-oriented approach to technology and to different sociopolitical systems and their modes of production, what they have at times overlooked is the fact that it was non-renewable fossil fuels that made possible in the first place what has often been referred to as "industrial civilization," or what Mark Blumler (2008) has called "the great experiment." Given that the non-renewable resources on which this experiment was based are becoming more and more difficult and costly to extract, it is surely safe to say that the next great experiment will be one in which the transition to renewable resources is the crucial task; after all, our civilization cannot continue to exist in its current form without an uninterrupted supply of energy.

In his well-known reconstruction of the early stages of human history, Leslie White (1949) noted that people originally utilized their muscles as a source of energy, eventually supplementing this through the domestication and use of animals (methods still widely in use around the world even today). With the agricultural revolution and the end of nomadic ways of life, the first human settlements were founded on the use of energy from plants and food crops. In the next stage described by White, human communities learned to extract and use natural resources, such as coal and oil. Writing in the 1940s, White saw nuclear energy as the next important step (like many others at that time, he adopted an uncritical stance towards this energy source). Whether or not White was correct in his historical reconstruction of human history as a history of energy expansion (from human muscles to nuclear power), it appears to be inevitable that the twenty-first century will bring yet another energy transition – or expansion – if highly industrialized societies are to survive. What this also points to, however, is a marked decline in existing sources of energy, something White did not discuss. Coal, gas, and oil will not be available forever, and the impacts (both in the present and over the very long term) of nuclear power appear to be increasingly unacceptable to many citizens so that the next transition will involve discarding existing practices and technologies of energy utilization on the household as well as the industrial level. This can be understood as a process of "exnovation" – the reverse side of the innovation-oriented view of progress at the end of the nuclear or fossil fuel age – in which existing forms of energy utilization are discarded in order to enable the emergence of new and experimental forms of energy utilizing activities. Although the use of the term exnovation varies in different contexts, we take it to refer in general terms to processes that steer the energy transition towards greater sustainability, that is, towards processes that open up greater possibilities for the well-being of future generations and the integrity of ecological systems over extended periods of time. This would involve ruling out practices, technologies, and forms of energy utilization that lead to unsustainable processes (see Paech 2013, Sveiby *et al.* 2012).

In one of the earliest attempts to define exnovation, organization theorist John Kimberly described it as a practice that is located at the very end of a multi-stage innovation process, in fact as "the removal of an innovation from an organization. Exnovation occurs when an organization divests itself of an innovation in which it had previously invested" (Kimberly 1981: 91). Kimberly stresses that exnovation may differ from merely discontinuing use of an innovation; exnovation implies active rejection of an innovation that has been invested in previously. Abstracting from the organizational level on which Kimberly focuses, we can say that, although there is much debate about when fossil fuels will effectively be used up (i.e. whether global peak oil has already been reached or whether it is still a few decades away), hardly anybody seriously doubts that accessible fossil fuels will eventually be depleted and that a "business as usual" take on energy utilization is no longer tenable for a variety of sociocultural, economic, political, and ecological reasons. In short, exnovation may soon become a question of necessity rather than one of choice. From a sociological point of view, a further crucial point to bear in mind is that increasing energy consumption does not automatically lead to an increase in quality of life (Buttel 1978, Mazur and Rosa 1974, Rosa *et al.* 1988); on the contrary, it has the potential to lead toward societal collapse. Thus, efforts aimed at simply reducing the side effects of energy consumption by achieving energy efficiency may not be helpful. Indeed, as Richard York (2012) has argued, implementing efficiency measures and finding substitutes for traditional energy sources often do not lead to the intended outcome when net effects are considered. This further underlines our argument that both innovation and exnovation in energy transformation processes need to be conceptualized as part of sociotechnical systems embedded in public policy and governance. In this sense, they can be conceptualized as social innovations (Howaldt *et al.* 2014, Rückert-John 2013) that are able to meet people's needs and support their well-being in an environmentally sustainable manner.

IGNORANCE AND EXPERIMENT: IRONIC PERSPECTIVE IN SOCIOLOGY

The following pages in this book describe the processes entailed in transitioning from one form of energy supply (known variously as fossil fuels or non-renewable energies) to a different one (known collectively as renewables) as an inherent challenge for understanding the world in the twenty-first century and developing theories about it for this purpose. Social and technological processes of transition have been addressed by virtually all the classical sociologists and can thus be regarded as a core theme of sociology *per se*.

In this book, therefore, we will not only discuss specific examples of local experimentation in energy transition but will also shed light on the broader and longer term processes of the "next great experiment" in energy transition. This will be done first by attending to classical as well as contemporary views on energy issues, beginning with Herbert Spencer's musings on energy and society and moving on to consider, among others, Max Weber's reflections on the role of energy supply in the rise and continued dominance of capitalism.

This will be followed by a look at recent developments in transition management in sociology and related fields, which seek to provide an explanatory context for processes of transformation ranging from everyday practices and niche experimentation to large-scale economic and political processes underway in modern societies.

Second, the book will situate recent attempts to change forms of energy consumption at the national level within longer standing debates about phasing out nuclear power. Amidst a recent backslide in many countries towards increasing reliance on coal to generate electricity, such debates include attempts to demonstrate that renewables can fill the nuclear gap quickly enough and in a cost-effective way, thereby forestalling an otherwise inexorable return to coal. In this context it is important to consider the unintended consequences, unpleasant surprises, and rebound effects triggered by attempts to transform contemporary energy systems to renewable ones – not least because given that this great experiment cannot be controlled, such attempts may lead to lock-in effects, adverse developments, and possibly even a return to the agricultural stage of modern societies. In sum, the issue of energy can be understood in sociological terms as the lynchpin in our understanding of the way societies – indeed modernity and progress in general – are set to develop in the twenty-first century. Given that the expansion of renewables will not occur proportionately to the phase out of fossil fuel-based energy use, the experimental transition from a mainly fossil fuel-based energy system to a world of renewable energy will require not just technological change but also sociocultural transformation.

On the basis of this understanding, experiments and unexpected sociotechnical change share some crucial similarities. An experiment can be defined in the most general sense as a cautiously observed venture into the unknown. An experiment is deliberately arranged to generate unexpected events and the surprising effects derived from the experimental set up can be seen as the driver behind the production of new knowledge, not least because surprises help the experimenter to become aware of their ignorance. If an experiment has failed and the hypothesis has been falsified, then the experimenter has been successful (see Brock 2010). This can be related to what Louis Schneider once called the ironic perspective in sociology. An ironic perspective often fosters a "wry smile just because one witnesses the bafflement or mockery of the fitness of things, of their supposed-to-be character" (Schneider 2012: 324). Put differently, most social processes involve an element of surprise, where the consequences can be the opposite of what was originally intended. The crucial difference is that such surprises or "failures" in a laboratory experiment, when greeted with a "wry smile," are welcomed and can even be considered as successes, whereas in contemporary processes of energy transition they normally are not. In the real world, failures are to be avoided, of course. This book therefore also seeks to locate the planned unexpectedness of experiments and the governance of ignorance at the heart of current strategies to establish greater use of renewable energy.

Given that the acknowledgement of ignorance is a crucial element in processes of experimentation, ignorance cannot be thought of simply as the absence of knowledge. If this were the case, it would clearly be judged to be an undesirable condition. Scholars in many disciplines have recently begun to challenge this negative assumption, exploring the ways in which ignorance can be more than simply the obverse of knowledge. Such inquiries have demonstrated that ignorance has a social and political life of its own (for an overview, see Gross and McGoey 2015). They have pointed out that in many areas of social life, individuals often need to act in spite of (sometimes) well-defined ignorance, or what has more recently been termed nonknowledge – the possibility of becoming knowledgeable about the specifics of one's own ignorance (Gross 2010a, 2012). Unlike the notion of ignorance, nonknowledge refers to knowledge about what is not known but is reasonably well defined. Nonknowledge constitutes a more precise form of the unknown and can thus be used when describing how decisions are made that have an uncertain outcome. It can also point to mechanisms of control relating to what ought (or ought not) to be known.[1] Nonknowledge will therefore be referred to when discussing the experimental strategies involved in advancing towards a post-fossil fuel and (hopefully) renewable energy society along with the inevitable knowledge gaps they entail.

One crucial issue associated with such experimental processes is that in many theoretical conceptualizations of the energy transition, there has been no clear focus on the connection between energy sources and the socioeconomic development of societies. From the first Industrial Revolution onwards, the use of fossil fuels has been closely interrelated with the development of high energy societies in terms of production and consumption. Lewis Mumford (1934) distinguished between the pre-industrial (or "eco-technological") state of early industrial society based on the utilization of energy from plant crops, wood, and hydropower and the "neo-technical" state of high industrialization in which electrical energy flows through all parts of society.

The present challenge is to effect a sociotechnical transition to a low energy society based on alternative energies and sustainable patterns of consumption. Whereas the first industrial experiment was a fossil fuel revolution, the "next great experiment" will need to be based on a sociotechnical transition to renewable energy use. The book will therefore discuss theoretical approaches that address the stabilization as well as the destabilization and transformation of sociotechnical systems. This will be linked to current debates on energy conflicts and the culturally rooted specificities of people's acceptance of renewable energy. Studies conducted since the 1970s have shown that although novel technologies may increase the efficiency of energy throughput, actual reductions in energy use are dependent on what may sometimes be tiny differences in culturally rooted practices. They depend, for example, on the everyday habitual practices of users rooted in different kinds of personal relationships within the household (see Bartiaux and Salmón 2014, Brand 2010, Shove 2004, Wilhite 2014).

SOCIOLOGY AND THE IDEA OF RENEWABLE ENERGY

From a sociological perspective, current energy debates are crucial and unique for at least two major reasons: (1) they point to a phase of transition from one major type of energy production to another and to a concomitant transformation of forms of social organization and (2) this transition will leave no social subsystem unaffected. Part of this entails the generation of new discourses on the foundations of social order, from the democratization of science and engineering to transparency in decision-making in connection with the inherent uncertainties involved in the utilization of new energy sources. Another part has to do with the reordering of social structures in connection with a change from centralized energy distribution to decentralized modes of energy production, which, in turn, gives rise to fundamental shifts in social organization that affect all areas of people's lives.

A further issue exists that has a key impact on contemporary debates in the social sciences and in sociology in particular. Most classical authors were convinced by the second law of thermodynamics – the law of entropy – which states that in a closed system differences in temperature, for example, will achieve equilibrium over time. Rudolf Clausius had shown in 1854 that heat could not pass from a cooler body to a hotter one without some external influence, such as an external heating device (see Roy 2002). Since then, physicists have shown that the energy depletion associated with the entropy of an energy system applies only to closed systems. The Earth, however, needs to be conceptualized as an open system that is receiving a constant flow of solar energy, energy that can be used efficiently and stored before flowing back into space. In order for humanity to survive, it is important therefore to use more and more of this ever-flowing renewable energy from above and, increasingly, from below the Earth's crust as well.

More generally speaking, energy supply constitutes a crucial strategic foundation of modern societies. Securing access to it over time is a key task for ensuring the survival of any society. This being the case, it ought to be considered just as important as other areas of sociological research and policy, and yet it is not. The structuration of energy access is a complex problem that touches on many areas of science and engineering. Knowledge about access to energy and the development of innovative new technologies are interlinked with economic and political processes as well as with cultural patterns of energy use.

Additionally, energy is, in many ways, a special field of study. Most importantly, one cannot produce or create energy but can only transform it from one source into another. A power plant does not produce energy (or "power") but rather transforms it, as when nuclear energy, for example, is transformed into electrical energy. To take another example, the combustion engine converts chemical energy into mechanical or kinetic energy. Despite this, terms such as power generation or energy production are widely used and accepted so that it is difficult not to make use of them (as we ourselves do in the remainder of this book). Furthermore, every process of energy conversion entails losses that are known as waste heat. These losses can be very significant, as in traditional incandescent light bulbs where over 95 percent of energy is turned into heat and only a small part is converted into visible light. Energy is not something that simply disappears or "evaporates," it is merely transformed either by itself or by human activity and is thus always a part of social life. This recalls Barry Commoner's well-known assertion that everything must go somewhere. As he notes, there is no waste in the natural world and, more importantly, there is no "away" where things can simply be thrown (see Commoner 1971). Viewed this way, energy is an inherent, intrinsic aspect of social change. Energy can therefore be seen not only as the glue that holds together different elements of the social order but also as a force that helps to transform them (or hinder their transformation) and to facilitate the creation of new social arrangements. One of the most pressing issues of our time is how to satisfy the growing and changing energy needs of societies in every corner of the world and, in particular, how to transform raw energy into electric or mechanical power in the most effective way.

Renewable energy – sometimes known also as alternative or sustainable energy – generally refers to available energy sources that constitute an alternative to fuel-based sources while avoiding the perceived negative consequences of using fuels (fossil or otherwise).

Renewable energy sources can be divided into three major groups. The primary sources of renewable energy are (1) the sun, a natural fusion reactor that produces energy through nuclear fusion; (2) the gravitational forces of the sun and the moon, the mechanical energy effects of which are generated from the power of the tides and waves, as well as by wind energy (the latter in connection with different heat levels between land and sea or plains and mountains); and (3) geothermal energy, which originates partially from the heat generated during the formation of the planet and, to a much greater extent (some 80 percent), from the radioactive decay of minerals in subterranean layers of the Earth (see Table 1.1). All of these types of renewable energy sources entail various challenges in sociocultural, political, and economic terms (see Horta *et al.* 2014). Our focus for the remainder of this book is on transition-related challenges and their sociological implications for twenty-first-century societies, particularly with regard to the switch from fossil and nuclear energy to energy drawn from the sun, gravitation, or the Earth's heat.

Although energy issues have a long tradition in sociology and other social sciences, they have never been central to any social science discipline. In the nineteenth century, most social science approaches to energy merely discussed the substitution of human labor by technology as an indicator of progress. Until recently, the main indicator used – at least implicitly – to measure the level of a country's civilization was consumption per capita. During most of the twentieth century, it was this way of thinking that lead to an almost reckless consumption of fossil fuels and non-renewable energy sources. The cheap access to oil enjoyed by the major industrialized countries to date has led to very high levels of resource consumption. One of the derivative products of oil, plastic, is widely seen nowadays as a symbol of waste and consumption in what US publicist Vance Packard (1960) once referred to as "the throwaway society." Even as many contemporary authors emphasize the achievements of modern industrial civilization, forged by overcoming the energy limitations of agricultural societies, they are also increasingly aware of and concerned to explore the limits set by environmental degradation caused by the depletion of energy resources.

In this book, we will focus on the importance of the transition-related aspects of alternative energy generation and consumption in order to better understand some of the challenges encountered on our path towards what are often government-led "energy turnarounds." We do so by focusing on theories of energy use and energy transition as a means of providing an accessible overview of the relationships between different types of energy production and their practical uses in modern societies. The specific approach taken in this book is to evaluate different types of energy production in terms of their mutual relations and to show how renewable energy sources can best be understood as rooted in their cultural and social contexts. The

Table 1.1 Types of renewable energy use and their sociological implications

Source	Examples of uses	Type of energy	Examples of sociological challenges
Sun	Thermal collectors, photovoltaic solar power plants, biomass/biogas power plants, wind energy through geographical differences in temperature levels, etc.	Electrical and thermal energy.	Transition from centralized to decentralized system structures, integration of renewable energies into existing energy structures or replacement of these, social conflicts, rebound effects, environmental governance, etc.
Gravitation	Tidal and wave power plants, wind energy converters.	Mainly electrical energy.	Transition from centralized to decentralized system structures, socio-technical system integration, aesthetic issues related to onshore and offshore wind farms, social conflicts, participation, etc.
Geothermal	Geothermal power plants, heat pumps, etc.	Electrical and thermal energy from deep geothermal sources, mainly thermal heat from shallow sources (household level)	Transition from centralized to decentralized system structures, unforeseen (seismic and economic) risks and conflict issues, sociocultural reservations, etc.

argument put forward in this regard is not that a single valid truth will be found by achieving certainty through science, but that political processes should be designed so as to generate favorable conditions for experimenting with ways of handling unavoidable ignorance and surprise. These might include, for instance, practices that give people the freedom to experiment with new forms of energy utilization and distribution and to reshape existing sociotechnical infrastructures, possibly even creating new, alternative systems.

NOTE

1 Complete unknowns constitute a different epistemic category to the notion of nonknowledge and have also been referred to as "ignorance squared" (Smithson 1985), "nescience" (Gross 2010a) and, perhaps most prominently, as "unknown unknowns" (Böschen 2009, Grove-White 2001, Kerwin 1993).

2

ENERGY AND SOCIETY

ENERGETIC FOUNDATIONS
OF SOCIOLOGY

This chapter discusses a number of ways of theorizing issues to do with energy and society, starting with the work of Herbert Spencer in the nineteenth century and progressing to more-recent approaches. This historical overview is important as a means of theoretically contextualizing current energy-related issues, ranging from recent political decisions, such as the proclaimed energy transitions in several European countries and beyond, to other energy transition approaches, such as "clean coal" rhetoric or debates around a sustainable green economy in many parts of the world.

Although power is a crucial concept for many social scientists, the term is most commonly used to refer to the social, economic, or cultural influences exerted by particular individuals or groups over other groups; it is rarely addressed as a concept referring to physical power or energy, not to mention power as the rate at which energy is used or transformed. Although sociological attempts to include matters "energetic" in theorizing society have a relatively long history, debates on energy as a transformative feature of social processes, modernity, progress, globalization, and social differentiation have only recently attracted the attention of some sociologists.

EVOLUTIONISM, ENERGETIC DETERMINISM, AND HUMAN ECOLOGY

One of the founding fathers of sociology, British philosopher, biologist, and political theorist Herbert Spencer (1820–1903), discussed in his *Principles of Sociology* (1896 [1876]) the continuous utilization of new forms of energy as a fundamental prerequisite for social evolution. In general, he felt that the development of human societies could be "measured by the degree in which simple acquisition is replaced by production; achieved first by manual power, then by animal power, and finally by machine power" (Spencer 1896 [1876]: 356, volume 3). Spencer raised questions about both the potential and the limitations of energy drawn from the natural environment to power societal development. Given that biological processes were the inspiration for this approach, it was inevitable that subsequent debates would focus on questions such as whether cultures develop in the same way as organisms and whether they embody parallels to the processes of natural selection and mutation identified by Charles Darwin. Spencer's organic conception of society assumes that a typical society consists of a group of individuals who live and work together and that it is just as much a unity (despite being made up of individuals) as is the animal or plant composed of cells and differentiated into mutually dependent tissues and organs (see Gross 2003: 79–81). As Andrew McKinnon (2010) argues, all historical and sociological reconstructions undertaken by Spencer in his oeuvre are driven by the underlying idea that different forms of energy production and consumption need to be seen as the basis for global and local trade in goods, as well as for movements of people. Thus, from this early sociological perspective, physical power and energy is regarded not as something that is "tacked onto" society and social development, but as the actual driving force behind it. In this functionalist understanding of society, Spencer concluded that the pressures of selection force societies to shape and accommodate their internal structure by means of differentiation in response to external resource shortages or new possibilities, such as hitherto untapped energy sources. Perhaps the most interesting part of Spencer's work in relation to the energy issues of today, however, is that his notion of evolution was not linear.

In other words, each new decision in politics and each new techno-logical development arises not only out of the failure of previous decisions but is, in turn, the catalyst for new failures – something he often referred to as selection pressures – that threaten society's sur-vival. Thus, for Spencer, unintended setbacks appear to be a normal part of social development. On this basis he suggested that human societies were best left to their natural inclinations. His view of the appropriate role of political and reformist activity ruled out actions by the state to improve social life (see Gross 2010a: 15). If we extend our interpretation of Spencer's ideas regarding energy a little further, we can say that energy in the form of physical power is to be under-stood as a kind of uncontrollable determinant to which societies are simply exposed and to which they passively adapt. Spencer was not alone in this respect. Many other authors of the late nineteenth and early twentieth centuries sought to conceptualize the energetic foun-dations of society and, in some cases, even attempted to develop cultural theories of energy.

One adherent of Spencer's conception of society was German sociologist and economist Albert Schäffle (1831–1903). Schäffle took Spencer's general analogy between the biological and the social as his point of departure but modified and elaborated the particular analo-gies within what Spencer had termed the social organism. Schäffle's basic perspective was that:

> empirically all changes are manifested as the consequence of the uni-versal interaction between the simplest and the composite parts of the universal whole of nature, an interaction that is expressed physi-cally as gravity, the influence of heat and light and chemical affinity, and biologically and sociologically as nervous energy, language, transport etc.
>
> (Schäffle 1878: 20; our translation)

Schäffle defined society as "a complex consisting of persons and things outside the human body" (Schäffle 1878: 18). He was also much less given to the Spencerian type of analogical reasoning. Although Schäffle came much closer to the view that the organic bond linking the members of a society to one another was essentially of a psychic nature, he nevertheless regarded social processes as similar to (albeit more complex than) biological process. This approach can most generally be characterized as a position that locates the origin of the social in the character of the natural world. In both Schäffle's and Spencer's conception of society, the natural environment and the utilization of energy as a social cause merged into a perspective that could be called evolutionist because a good deal of the sociological thinking of the time was overwhelmingly influenced by Darwinian ideas.

Perhaps best known today in this respect is Wilhelm Ostwald (1853–1932), even if it is mainly for the Nobel Prize in chemistry that he received in 1909 and for the criticism he received from Max Weber (1909) for his book *Energetische Grundlagen der Kulturwissenschaft* [*Energetic Foundations of the Cultural Sciences*] (1909). Quite contrary to contemporary sociological approaches to modern society, Ostwald promoted his theory of energetics as an underlying principle of all aspects and subsystems of society. Building on Immanuel Kant's categorical imperative, Ostwald (1911) outlined his energetic imperative in a way that might be summarized as "waste no energy, utilize it!" What Ostwald sought to accomplish in his sociological treatise of 1909 was to apply his energetic imperative to the issue of human labor and to all aspects of social progress and development. In the book's foreword he states that he originally planned the book with the word "sociology" in its title but then decided that "cultural science" (*Kulturwissenschaft*) would be the more fitting term. Furthermore, he claimed that his book would be "the foundation of sociology from the point of view of energetics." After all, as Ostwald continues, "Under no circumstances, however, can sociology exempt itself from the task of examining its problems in the light of energetics" (Ostwald 1909: 3; our translation). He argued further that energy efficiency should provide the underlying rationale for modern society. By so doing Ostwald highlighted the fact that every major cultural change is based on new energy sources or major shifts in energy utilization due to the need to satisfy technological societies' ever-increasing demand for energy. Although Ostwald's clearly deterministic and naturalistic take on culture and society from an energetic point of view did not receive much attention from sociologists subsequently, it is his approach to the issue that still makes his views instructive today in relation to the current challenge of incorporating energetic issues into sociological theories of society in the twenty-first century.

The problem Ostwald faced with the deterministic notion of energy as an explanatory variable for all things cultural can also be found typologically in other areas of the social sciences. Even Emile Durkheim – often referred to as one of the most "socio-centric" authors of the classical tradition on account of his dictum to analyze social facts using only other preceding social facts – understood society as a part of nature when he wrote that a:

> society is the most powerful combination of physical and moral forces of which nature offers us an example. Nowhere else is an equal richness of different materials, carried to such a degree of concentration, to be found. Then it is not surprising that a higher life disengaged itself which, by reacting upon the elements of which it is the product, raises them to a higher plane of existence and transforms them.
>
> (Durkheim 1947: 446)

Not only could this statement easily have come from organicists such as Spencer or Schäffle, but Durkheim also proposes that human society is nothing other than a continuation of nature. It is just a higher expression of the same energies that underlie all natural phenomena, except that society is higher in the hierarchy than the rest of nature. Furthermore, Durkheim based his explanation of differentiation in society on the fact of population increase and on the problems arising from this due to limited space as well as to differential access to natural resources.

While the significance of energy for understanding the way societies develop was not a marginal topic, it was often treated as merely secondary in sociological analysis. Nonetheless, the topic has been discussed widely in the sociological tradition by scholars as diverse as the previously mentioned chemist turned sociologist Wilhelm Ostwald (1909), geographer Ellsworth Huntington (1924), historian, urban sociologist, and philosopher Lewis Mumford (1934), and later also by economists and mathematicians such as Nicholas Georgescu-Roegen (1971), as well as anthropologists such as Richard Adams (1975) and the previously mentioned Leslie White (1949). Adopting a similar approach to Spencer's, these scholars pointed to the causal connection between different modes of energy utilization and the level or state of civilization of a certain society or nation state, as well as the respective power relations that went hand-in-hand with these types of development. White, for instance, argued that the primary goal for any society is to capture more energy than competing societies and to use it more efficiently in order to gain advantage over other societies. In his classical book *The Science of Culture* (1949), White goes so far as to state that the amount of energy a society can capture is the appropriate indicator by which to judge the level of civilization it has reached. This view, which was also held by many sociologists of the early twentieth century, was not formulated arbitrarily. Both in the United States and in Europe sociology emerged at that time as an intellectual response to industrialization, urbanization, the increasing division of labor, and the exploitation of natural resources brought about by these developments. Indeed sociological speculation about the role of the environment in and for society is as old as the discipline itself. However, as we saw previously, across most of nineteenth-century social thought, the impact of nature on society was perceived as deterministic. Some social science scholars of the time – especially geographers – were guided by the view that environments shape cultures, that is, not only that geographical factors determine cultural characteristics but also that these factors act directly upon cultures. This geographical, or environmental, determinism addressed questions of how cultural features originate, change, adapt, and how they function in the broader society. One such well-known author in the early twentieth century was geographer Ellsworth Huntington (1876–1947). Huntington believed that natural environments and access to the energy resources contained in these environments shape culture. This view made it possible to explain all manner of (perceived) cultural features; moreover, it accounted for cultural diversity by referring to the influences exerted by the natural environment. Thus, one primary issue for some thinkers of the late nineteenth and early twentieth centuries with regard to the energy potential of the material environment was not so much the origins of environmental degradation and environmental problems, but the way in which societies are held in check by their natural environment. A famous example of this type of energetic – here, climatic – determinism was the work by Huntington on the relationship between climate and the degree of civilization of a nation. Although a geographer by training, Huntington also published in sociological textbooks and journals, and his geographical findings were influential for many of the sociologists of his time. In his classical treatise *Civilization and Climate* (1924), he argued that the level of civilization reached across the globe could be related to the amount of available energy determined by different climatic zones (Huntington 1924: 240ff.). This finding was based on questionnaires that Huntington had distributed to scientists around the world in 1913 in order to rate the level of civilization in their country. Huntington's fundamental thesis was that changes in temperature and climate also determine the ebb and flow of civilizations. His development of "a geographic basis of history" included four main classes of factors. The first was differences in the distribution of water and temperature from north to south. The second was natural changes, accidental occurrences such as earthquakes, volcanic eruptions, and, especially, rapid climatic changes. The third was the doctrine of sunspots as a factor in periodic climatic changes. Huntington went on to prove that more sunspots also mean more storms, hence changes in sunspots lead to shifts in what he called the storm belt. The last element Huntington identified was the notion that the whole world can be characterized in terms of pulsating climate changes (Huntington 1924: 275ff.). The important point here is that, in Huntington's view, climate has a direct effect upon social development and that it also has a strong indirect but "immediate effect through food and other resources, through parasites, and through mode of life" (Huntington 1924: 3). As influential as Huntington's and others' findings were in their lifetimes, this mechanistic linking of society to energetic issues did not fit well with observations and evidence.

The notion of viewing societies in their ecological context was also prominent in the early development of the so-called Chicago School of Sociology in the first few decades of the twentieth century. Some of these debates were gathered together in an influential introductory textbook by Robert E. Park and Ernest Burgess (1972), but the topic was further developed by authors such as Roderick McKenzie (1926). In this Chicago approach, it was not only the territorial aspect of society but also the dimension of time and ecological processes that came to the fore (see MacDonald 2011). The central thesis of this approach – referred to as human ecology, a term originally introduced by Ellen Swallow Richards (1907) drawing on the ideas of Ernst Haeckel (1866) – was that in many respects human societies can be adequately understood only by studying their component communities in the light of the specific material environment in which they are located. The principal assertion is that the development of any society is inseparable from the dynamics of its natural environment. Thus, human ecology was implicitly regarded as the study of whatever ecosystems included humans. Roderick McKenzie summarizes what he refers to as the processual nature of the ecological complex as follows: "In society physical structure and cultural characteristics are part of one complex. The spatial and sustenance relations in which human beings are organized are ever in a process of change in response to the operation of a complex of environmental and cultural forces" (McKenzie 1926: 141). Park and Burgess, and McKenzie were not alone in this view. The importance of the interaction between humans and their material environment can be found in many works by early sociologists. Edward A. Ross (1866–1951), another classical American sociologist of the early twentieth century, attempted to tackle the problem of one-sided energetic explanations by putting forward the idea of external (ecological, geographical) and social controls (Ross 2009). Ross attempted to define the scope of sociology by taking a midway position between the nineteenth-century organicist theory of sociologists like Herbert Spencer and the focus on subjective human behavior, as proclaimed by sociology in the mid-twentieth century. Ross rejected the idea that sociology should focus on any single factor. He believed that sociology should incorporate units of analysis that lend themselves to empirical investigation and the discovery of causation. The result was a sociological paradigm in which society is in a reciprocal relationship with its natural environment and so must constantly adjust in response to both natural and social conditions in order to maintain its coherence and continue to develop. Thus, to sum up Ross's all-encompassing notion of control, "social" control might acquire greater importance in the modern world, but it would always be just one part of the explanatory equation (see Gross 2010b). Energy supply (or the preliminary processes, as Ross sometimes called them) is the basis of society, which in turn effects modifications in nature through social processes. Ross had an awareness of the reciprocal relationship between society and nature and the importance of including natural processes and energy resources in any description of social change. In his view, human societies remain immersed in the dynamic processes of nature, even as they appear to control it.

ENERGY UTILIZATION AND THE RISE OF CAPITALISM

The most prominent classical European author of sociology to discuss the natural environment in relation to energy issues was Max Weber (1864–1920).[1] Despite Weber's proposition of a *verstehende* sociology, the material environment played a pivotal role in his understanding of the rise of capitalism, particularly in his historical writings. In his discussion of the previously mentioned book by Ostwald on the energetic foundations of sociology, Weber argues resolutely against any one-sided explanation of the sociocultural realm based on energy issues. Nevertheless, he reminds his readers "that sociologists need to be clear that the physical and chemical energy balance is part of the design of processes of technical and economic development." Weber goes on to stress that, "all causal influences derived from the application of the laws of energy need to be taken carefully into account when seeking to understand social phenomena" (Weber 1909: 596; our translation).

Taking the subjective perspective of individual social actors as his starting point, Weber describes in the early pages of *Economy and Society* (1978) how the social and physical environment appears as a predefined structure. It is people's subjective projections of meaning that construct the significance of these structures. Natural resources or "energetic causes," as Weber (1909) called them in reference to Ostwald, were not to be understood as determining influences but were instead to be considered as sociologically relevant causal influences at specific turning points in the development of capitalism. Ecological factors and the use of technology were not determinate for Weber, and yet he recognized that they played an important role through their interaction with social factors such as religious norms, the economy, political decision making, warfare, and the emergence of complex social structures in general. According to Weber, the exploitation and consequent exhaustion of natural resources need to be conceptualized as crucial along the trajectory of industrial development.

It is interesting to note that in his non-professional life too, Weber did not treat the natural world and modes of energy production as merely marginal. His participation in the first German nature protection association, the *Bund für Heimatschutz*, may serve as a reliable indicator of this. Together with some 1,500 artists, writers, and scientists, Weber protested against the building of a hydropower plant in the River Rhine near Laufenburg as an act of landscape destruction (Sieferle 1986). Given this, it is no wonder that the "destruction of nature" or, as he sometimes termed it, the "pillage economy," was discussed at length in some of his writings on the Protestant ethic. This resonates clearly with some of the more pessimistic writings of Weber's friend and colleague Georg Simmel (1998). In his famous essay entitled "The Concept and Tragedy of Culture" (orig. 1911), Simmel diagnosed the evolution of science and technology as tragic because, with increasing progress, their achievements may appear to us as uncontrollable "objective" powers that in some cases lead towards decadence or decline. This evolutionary development can also generate senseless new needs in technological developments and the utilization of energy sources. Simmel's example, with reference to the autonomous development of modern science, is that although "no one would find it useful to drill for coal or gas at random anywhere in the world" (1998: 213), someone might nonetheless be inspired to do so, given that the chance of something being found is inherent in the character of modern scientific research. In Simmel's view, human societies are powerless in the face of their own technological accomplishments because the latter may often develop quite independently of the will of their creators and no longer answer to the subjective energy needs of human well-being. Thus, Simmel implicitly highlighted the danger that modern science would arbitrarily support the production of energy that is not needed for the satisfaction of individual human needs. Taking this line of thinking a stage further, we might even detect here a nascent cautionary argument regarding the development of scientifically informed energy cartels that may generally tend to slow down the processes needed to imagine and devise novel forms of energy utilization.

Weber's particular concern, however, was to better understand the role of religion in social development and economic issues. In a chapter on the ascetic lifestyle in which Weber attempts to "understand the connection between the fundamental religious ideas of ascetic Protestantism and its maxims for everyday economic conduct" (2001: 102), he outlines the seemingly unavoidable dilemma of ecological destruction occurring as a result of modern modes of production:

> For when asceticism was carried out of monastic cells into everyday life, and began to dominate worldly morality, it did its part in building the tremendous cosmos of the modern economic order. This order is now bound to the technical and economic conditions of machine production which to-day determine the lives of all the individuals who are born into this mechanism, not only those directly concerned with economic acquisition, with irresistible force. Perhaps it will so determine them until the last ton of fossilized coal is burnt.
>
> (Weber 2001: 123)

Weber thus not only points to the danger of pillaging nature's resources, criticizing the "capitalist spirit" of his time, he also sensitizes his readers to an awareness of the outside world, referring to the English churchman Richard Baxter (1615–1691). The "light coat" of the material environment (external goods), which in a sustainable world should be rendered as taken for granted, can turn into a shell as hard as steel (*stahlhartes Gehäuse*) via the depletion of natural resources, and excessive energy use can develop into a fate as a result.

According to Weber, both Lutherans and the traditional Catholic Church originally had a negative attitude towards capitalist development. This attitude slowly began to loosen as workers and peasants began to enact more ascetic lifestyles, adopting rationalities that were originally practiced only by monks in monasteries, but which now belonged to everyday Protestant life:

> The religious life of the saints, as distinguished from the natural life, was – the most important point – no longer lived outside the world in monastic communities, but within the world and its institutions. This rationalization of conduct within this world, but for the sake of the world beyond, was the consequence of the concept of calling of ascetic Protestantism.
>
> (Weber 2001: 100)

Here we find the crux of Weber's understanding of the development of the spirit of capitalism: "Since asceticism undertook to remodel the world and to work out its ideals in the world, material goods have gained an increasing and finally an inexorable power over the lives of men as at no previous period in history" (Weber 2001: 124). The tension that developed out of this constellation for Weber is the following: the workers pursue their calling in a spirit of asceticism, through which their work ethic becomes linked to the logic of capitalism and growth. The logic of capitalism and growth, however, contradicts the biblical injunction to live a life of asceticism rather than indulgence. This tension between the Protestant ethic and the spirit of capitalism is expressed in relation to the natural environment as follows: on the one hand, the Protestant ethic calls for mindful stewardship of God's naturally given resources and for moderation in relation to consumption in general, while on the other hand, the ethic derived from the spirit of capitalism fosters the consumption of material goods and natural resources ("subdue the Earth"). Weber saw in the key elements of the spirit of capitalism and in its power to dictate certain habitual practices in everyday life an ascetic lifestyle, which in modern times has less and less to do with religion at all. Put differently, the Protestant ethic only becomes a problem when (in the absence of new discoveries of energy resources) the tension between asceticism and consumption leads to a depletion of fossilized fuels. The ongoing search for new forms of energy utilization is therefore a key element in Weber's work on the development of capitalism.

Explicitly religious ideas may, according to Weber, be the original drivers of certain types of social development. In the case of Europe however, religion was important mainly during the early stages of capitalist development, whereas in the course of its ongoing development, ecological, technical, and economic conditions became increasingly influential – including the imperative to discover ever new sources of energy. Taking the example of England, Weber shows that the introduction of new technologies and tools alone is not a sufficient explanatory variable for modern capitalism because "its victory was decided by coal and iron" – up until the eighteenth century "smelting and all preparation of iron was done with charcoal" (Weber 2003: 304), which had significant consequences in terms of the deforestation of large parts of England. Weber sums up:

> Everywhere the destruction of the forests brought the industrial development to a standstill at a certain point. Smelting was only released from its attachment to organic materials of the plant world by the application of coal. [...] In the face of the further development arose two difficult problems. These were set, on the one hand, by the danger of deforestation and, on the other, by the perpetual inroads of water in the mines. The first question was the more pressing because in contrast with the expansion of the textile industry the English iron industry had shrunk step by step until at the beginning of the 18th century it gave the impression of having reached its end. The solution to the problem was reached through the coking of coal.
>
> (Weber 2003: 304–5)

Thus, Max Weber was one of the first scholars to discuss the importance of modern processes of energy utilization in capitalist development and their role as a transformative element in energy production, given that all raw materials will run out at some point in time. His subsequent discussion shows even more clearly how significant the role was that he attributed to the discovery of alternative energy sources. Thus, he writes:

> In the first place, coal and iron released technology and productive possibilities from the limitations of the qualities inherent in organic

materials; from this time forward industry was no longer dependent upon animal power or plant growth. Through a process of exhaustive exploitation, fossil fuel, and by its aid iron ore, were brought up to the light of day, and by means of both men achieved the possibility of extending production to a degree which would have previously been beyond bounds of the conceivable.

(Weber 2003: 305)

According to Weber, however, such accomplishments do not give cause for complacency: iron can only be understood as yet another intermediate form of energy production in capitalist development because "the exploitative mining out of the underground wealth must have a limit in time [... T]he age of iron cannot last over a thousand years at most" (2003: 380). Although a thousand years appears to be a very long time, it is clear that, for Weber, there are likely to be no lasting, eternal solutions to the supply of energy and raw materials. For this reason, the continuous search for alternative resources on which to base capitalist development needs to be understood as a crucial factor in relation to "phenomena which are devoid of meaning," as Weber referred to the non-social entities with which humans interact in his famous introductory chapter to *Economy and Society* (Weber 1978: 4). It is interesting to note here that Weber, paradoxically very much in line with Ostwald, implicitly argues that every major cultural and social turnaround or shift is determined by novel methods of energy utilization, such as the continuous discovery of new energy sources. One can thus conclude that, to Weber's way of thinking, the development of capitalism needs to be conceptualized sociologically as a cyclical return to the energetic foundations of modern societies.

ENVIRONMENTAL SOCIOLOGY AND THE ENERGY QUESTION

Following on from Weber and others, in the middle of the twentieth century US sociologist Fred Cottrell (1903–1979) sought to revitalize energy-oriented sociology, albeit again without leaving any great impression on mainstream sociology. This is unfortunate because

Cottrell, unlike many of his predecessors, actually intended to develop a sociological theory based on transitions in energy availability and their link to the development of society and technology in general. His most well-known book is titled *Energy and Society* (1955). Cottrell not only analyzed the role of energy utilization (energy surpluses and returns) in the development of modern societies; what makes his work relevant even in the twenty-first century is his emphasis on the centrality of energy transitions (such as the transition from human labor and domestic animals to inanimate energy sources and their conversion to energy in the combustion engine) for the future of society. In 2009, 30 years after Cottrell's death, a revised edition of *Energy and Society* was published (Cottrell 2009). Cottrell had revised the book over the years, especially after the first oil crisis in 1973, but did not manage to publish it within his own lifetime. In a rewritten foreword, Cottrell stresses again that in the long run, societies with a large energy surplus have greater opportunities for progress and expansion. He thus makes a direct link between standard of living and different types of energy surpluses.

Despite these important predecessors, one can generally say that mainstream sociology, along with the other social sciences, have pursued an approach to explaining social phenomena that brackets out energy issues and instead freely follows the Durkheimian premise of explaining certain social facts by reference to other social facts. In addition to the attempts mentioned previously and those in the tradition of the Chicago School of human ecology and sociology, the need to include non-social phenomena in sociological research was expressed in a series of influential articles by North American sociologists William Catton and Riley Dunlap (e.g. Catton and Dunlap 1978). Here, Catton and Dunlap asserted their view that environmental sociology was a discipline-reshaping force of considerable importance. Their work also bore the implication that the theoretical divisions and concerns of sociology up to the 1960s and 1970s were beside the point. In other words, the environmental sociology of the 1970s was deliberately and quite understandably fashioned as a critique of mainstream sociology. The same can also be observed in Europe, especially in Germany – with authors such as Walter Bühl (1980) also proclaiming the rise of an ecological paradigm in sociology (though without making any reference to Catton, Dunlap, and others) – and later also in Britain and elsewhere (see Martell 1994).

The subdiscipline of environmental sociology thus emerged in North America only after what was generally understood as a wave of public environmental consciousness arose in the 1970s. The first oil crisis of 1973/74 in particular fostered sociological debate on the issue of resource scarcity and, as Riley Dunlap recalls (2011: 55–6), heightened people's awareness that the environment was more than yet another social problem to be tackled by sociologists. Energy shortages demonstrated that environmental conditions can indeed have direct social consequences, as well as the obvious fact that human activities are the reason for such shortages. From a sociological point of view, of course, it is one thing to register and analyze the discourse emerging from these types of resource shortages but it is quite another to integrate it into a social theory of interaction and communication. From the perspective of Weberian *verstehende* sociology, it is theoretically conceivable to go beyond attempts to take social actors' constructions of their own life world seriously and to actually place oneself as a sociological observer in the position of the "other." However, the problems that arise when trying to adopt the perspective of elemental phenomena, such as energetic forces or the growth of fauna and flora, storms, water, and fire, are truly formidable (see Gross 2014). Consequently, environmental sociology since the 1970s has sought to theorize the connection between human societies and the natural environment, albeit with a clear understanding that one-dimensional environmental determinist descriptions of society do not help in our understanding of environmental problems and disasters. In response to these public concerns, a separate section of the American Sociological Association devoted to environmental sociology was founded in 1976. Now the main focus shifted from "naturally given" impacts on social development to the impact of human transformations of the natural environment on human societies (human-induced global climate change, the smell of mountains of waste, contaminated industrial sites, etc.) which may, in turn, act back on human societies. Since its beginnings, environmental sociology has therefore placed its main emphasis on studying the dependency of social life and cultural development on our natural surroundings, on the factors that cause environmental problems, and on efforts to solve these problems.

The work of 1970s environmental sociology carried the implication that sociology should move towards a new ecological paradigm. This new paradigm was to challenge the alleged anthropocentrism of classical sociology by including environmental forces as objective variables in social explanations (see Catton and Dunlap 1978). In subsequent years, the notion of a new ecological paradigm has become a widely used measure of a pro-environmental orientation in sociology and other disciplines (see Stern *et al.* 1995). Despite being a relatively young subdiscipline, environmental sociology has produced a wide array of theoretical and empirical studies. There are, for example, studies on environmental awareness, sustainable consumption, ecological modernization, social movements, environmental justice, environmental communication, as well as numerous attempts at developing different social theories of society and its natural environment. Taken together, these strands of research convey the implicit notion that nature as a separate entity is in a "natural" state of balance and exists independently of human action. Consider the sociological notion of static nature. Even today, many environmental sociologists, as well some representatives of the classical tradition, adhere to the notion of an eternal nature that is in a steady state of fixed equilibrium. Indeed, at the end of the nineteenth century Emile Durkheim put it in quite explicit terms: "As for the physical world, since the beginning of history it has remained sensibly the same, at least if one does not take account of novel ties which are of social origin" (Durkheim 1933: 348). In other words, sociologists could easily bracket out any outside influence upon nature as an explanatory variable for social developments. As a result, changes in nature itself and the ways in which these changes might potentially act upon social constructions have not been considered to any great extent. This is no coincidence. Although the discipline of ecology has undergone a conceptual shift from an emphasis on ecosystem stability and balance to an acknowledgement of the importance of flux, chaos, and change in the natural world, this change – despite its profound implications being accepted in ecological restoration and conservation management – has generally remained beyond the awareness of the mainstream media and even of most social scientific literature (Gross 2003, Kricher 2009, Ladle and Gillson 2009). Indeed, many sociologists – at least implicitly – still portray the aim of the environmental sciences, ecology, and conservation efforts as being one of maintaining natural stability, harmony, and some type of natural balance. The ideal of balance in nature especially is still prominent in contemporary environmental thinking; in fact, for the most part it was a prerequisite for how environmental problems were to be defined and how their solutions should be envisaged. The idea of a balance in nature, so to speak, was seen not as a human desire but as a necessity imposed by nature. This is not surprising given that, although ecologists may perceive nature as existing in a constant state of change, for most people nature provides a source of stability and regularity – not least because in many respects it does appear stable (e.g. regularly changing seasons). Compared to social, economic, and cultural changes, natural changes sometimes appear to be miniscule (see Rautio 2011). Thus, while environmental thinking since the 1970s may appear rather novel, the ideas on which it is based represent a resurgence of early twentieth-century ecology blended with romantic myths about nature (see, for example, the musings of deep ecologists). In this view, undisturbed nature always achieves balance, constancy, and stability, while human beings simply interfere with and destroy that balance. Current public debates on nature conservation and "ecology" often have little to do with scientific ecology. To this end, the need for a new ecological paradigm makes even more sense (see Gross 2014).

In this regard, authors such as Lesley White (1949) and Fred Cottrell (1955) (discussed earlier) along with later scholars such as Craig Humphrey and Frederick Buttel (1982) have analyzed the different ways in which various subsystems of society are dependent on and intertwined with any given ecological or energetic influence. Social, cultural, and economic factors can be analyzed both as consequences and as sources of new forms of energy use. Whereas many authors seek to shed light on all these variables, in most cases single explanations are still prevalent. These range from geophysical factors such as access to coal or oil, technological innovations such as the steam engine or electric and combustion engines, economic factors such as a socialist or capitalist mode of production, as well as cultural factors such as modern Western lifestyles and value systems (see Nader 2010, Spreng et al. 2012, Strauss et al. 2013). The question that arises here is whether energy can be meaningfully described as a crucial indicator of social development and progress (energy as a causal variable) or whether classical social science analysis of the social and cultural factors leading to different types of energy usage is the more promising path. In this book, our emphasis is clearly on the classical sociological side. In other words, we use the social as an explanatory variable to analyze energy issues. If necessary, however, we do not shy away from using energy as a variable on a par with social facts to explain and analyze societal processes.

What all these studies and authors have in common is that they point to the sociological importance of analyzing energy utilization as a crucial element in understanding social development because without this part of the puzzle no society or political system can be adequately understood. Particularly in the case of Weber, we can see the important connection between capitalism, lifestyles, and work ethics, and the continuous search for new energy sources as a major driver of modernity and development. This connection will, in a way, be the crucial link to be discussed in the following chapters. Accordingly, in this book we focus on modern theories of energy in processes of sociotechnical transitions and on the centrality of these transitions in the search for new energy sources. We do so in order to stress the close interaction and connection between social and technological elements, such as cultural values, institutional settings, and political frameworks, and the everyday practices of heterogeneous actor constellations (see Rohracher 2008, Wilhite 2014). In this book, we take up various ideas from the classical writers and interweave them into our discussion of energy transitions and transition theory, using them as a point of reference throughout the remainder of the book.

NOTE

1 For a more general discussion of Weber's environmental sociology, see Gross (2001, chapter 2). A classical treatise of Weber's human ecology can be found in West (1985), while a recent reinterpretation can be found in Foster and Holleman (2012).

3

CONTEMPORARY SOCIAL THEORIES OF ENERGY TRANSITIONS

While the classical sociologists pointed mainly to the sociotechnical potential of altering modern societies' modes of production, since then the search for new energy sources has remained a marginal, poorly defined topic in sociological theory. Meanwhile, modern theories of sociotechnical transitions and related research activities have sought to develop explanatory frameworks capable of reflecting the fundamental fact that (capitalist) societies are characterized by constant socioeconomic change on the one hand, while also experiencing extended periods of techno-economic consolidation, stabilization, and growth on the other – something Max Weber referred to as the cyclical return to natural resources. In such periods, new sociotechnical regimes (e.g. the regime of energy supply) emerge, stabilize, and gain momentum, thus becoming the technological and infrastructural basis of societal development as well as its main driving force. However, when sociotechnical regimes decline and enter periods of destabilization or perhaps even fundamental transition, societal upheaval – if not foundational crises – can often be the result. Building on the "long wave" theories of global economic development (business cycles) introduced by Kondratiev and Schumpeter,

Christopher Freeman and Carlota Perez (1988), in a now classical essay, presented a theoretical concept that can be regarded as a path-breaking achievement in the field of evolutionary economics and the sociology of technical change.

A STRUCTURAL CRISIS OF ADJUSTMENT

According to many of the previously mentioned authors (including Leslie White, Fred Cottrell, and Richard Adams) any fundamental change in a longstanding techno-economic paradigm will necessarily be accompanied by "structural crises of adjustment." Freeman and Perez argue that such a "period of transition – the downswing and depression of the long wave – is characterized by deep structural change in the economy and such changes require an equally profound transformation of the institutional and social framework" (1988: 59). This transformation is "necessary to bring about a better 'match' between the new technology and the system of social management of the economy – or 'regime of regulation'" (1988: 38). Based on Kondratiev's famous concept of economic waves that last between 40 and 60 years and consist of alternating periods of growth and relative decline in the world economy (see Kondratiev 1926), Freeman and Perez outline a "tentative sketch of some of the main characteristics of successive long waves" (1988: 50): they distinguish five long waves between 1770/80 (the beginning of the Industrial Revolution) and 1980/90 (the emergence of a new "key factor industry" based on microelectronics). Each transition period within this wave – the point at which an "old" techno-economic paradigm declines and comes to be replaced by an emergent paradigm – is characterized by radical change in the *energetic foundations* of economy and society. While the first long wave of "early mechanization" (1770/80 to 1830/40) was based mainly on water power technologies, further developments in mechanization, expanding factory production, and rapid economic growth could only be achieved by a fundamental energy shift towards coal and steam power (second long wave from 1830/40 to 1880/90: "steam power and railway"). The next transition period and the subsequent rise of various new industries (e.g. production of heavy chemicals, steel ships, automobiles, air-craft, consumer durables) was driven by another fundamental change in the field of energy technology: the build-up of a comprehensive system of electricity supply and distribution (third long wave from 1880/90 to 1930/40: "electrical and heavy engineering"). The fourth long wave, characterized by "Fordist mass production" and mass consumption (1930/40 to 1980/90), was supported mainly by the rise of the oil industry, with oil becoming the dominant source of energy worldwide. According to Freeman and Perez's outline, a fifth long wave began around 1980/90 ("information and communication") – one that is still ongoing and that, in their view, is not associated with any new energy shift but rather with an (unre-marked) extension of the oil age. This is hardly surprising given that, in the late 1980s when Freeman and Perez wrote their article, there was no way of predicting the rise of alternative energies, let alone the "new" renewable energies. However, with regard to the succession of previous long waves, Freeman and Perez consider energy shifts nec-essary in order to overcome the mismatch between the emergent techno-economic paradigm and the old socio-institutional frame-work and technical infrastructure. Accordingly, periods of transition are also periods of re-accommodation:

> The re-accommodation occurs as a result of a process of political search, experimentation and adaptation, but when it has been achieved, by a variety of social and political changes at the national and international level, the resulting good 'match' facilitates the upswing phase of the long wave.
>
> (Freeman and Perez 1988: 59)

Freeman and Perez's approach is the result of a careful and complex analysis, and yet it includes a version of technological determinism in its explanatory framework for societal change. The authors con-ceptualize periods of transition in terms of the interdependent – and often conflict-ridden – co-development of emerging technologies, changing institutions, new societal values, forms of social behavior, and shifting relations between capital and labor. But when they speak of a "full-scale re-accommodation," the emerging techno-economic paradigm plays the role of an independent variable while re-accommodation occurs within institutions and societal structures, that is, at the level of societal values or in relation to political regulation and decision making.

GLOBAL ENERGY SHIFTS

While Freeman and Perez's explanation for the occurrence of long-term energy shifts favors the primacy of fundamental technological change, sociologist Bruce Podobnik (1999, 2006) opts for a genuine socio-historical approach in order to explain the "global energy shifts" that have occurred since the era of the Industrial Revolution. In short, Podobnik (2006) conceptualizes global energy shifts as outcomes of the "dynamics of geopolitical, commercial, and social competition." In a summary of his key conceptual tools, he states:

> Transitions from periods of world order to world chaos profoundly impact the global energy system. As this study will demonstrate, periods of relatively linear, predictable growth in energy systems are achieved during times when a hegemonic state is able to contain dynamics of geopolitical, commercial, and social competition within moderate frameworks. Conversely, periods of more profound change in global energy systems occur when hegemonic stability breaks down and the pressures of warfare, economic crisis, and social conflict can no longer be contained.
>
> (Podobnik 2006: 9)

In contrast to Freeman and Perez, Podobnik thus defines "global energy shift" as a dependent variable – as the result of a historically unique interplay of (geo)political, economic, and social conditions. Podobnik applies his approach to two key historic cases:

> Since the onset of the industrial revolution the world has in fact witnessed the full consolidation of two distinct energy regimes. The first, based upon coal, grew to maturity in the nineteenth century and then entered into relative stagnation in the twentieth century. The second, based upon petroleum, underwent global diffusion during the twentieth century but may be reaching maturity.
>
> (Podobnik 1999: 155)

Here is not the place to outline the complex historic circumstances described in detail by Podobnik in his analysis of each global energy shift (especially in Podobnik 2006). What is important to note, though, is that he sees the world at the outset of "a third global energy shift, towards a cluster of new energy technologies" (Podobnik 1999: 156), based mostly on natural gas and the various forms of renewable energies. Drawing on a projection, Podobnik (2006: 161) argues that natural gas will become the world's dominant energy source by around 2020, to be outpaced by renewable energies near the end of the twenty-first century. As in the case of the former coal regime and the currently ongoing oil regime, Podobnik (1999: 167) states that "the consolidation of a future energy regime" – now based "on a cluster of more sustainable technologies" – "will likely result from a similar convergence of geopolitical, commercial and social dynamics." Thus, he outlines a scenario under which a third global energy shift might be conceivable:

> If geopolitical and commercial competition for the world's remaining petroleum and natural gas resources intensifies as forecasted in the coming decades, and conflict continues to be endemic in the Middle East, the price of these resources will rise, and import-dependent states will have reasons to increase support for domestically-based alternative energy technologies. While increased state sponsorship of renewable energy technologies will also presumably reflect commitments made by nations throughout the world to limit the emissions of greenhouse gases, it is important to underscore the concrete political and commercial dynamics which are beginning to favor alternative energy sectors. It is also crucial to highlight the role of social movements in influencing the trajectory of world energy industries. Specifically, if environmental pressures on conventional energy industries can be increased throughout the world, then the comparative advantage of renewables would be heightened – stimulating a more rapid diffusion of alternative energy systems.
>
> (Podobnik 1999: 167)

This statement encompasses many assumptions about the long-term global energy future and the role of renewable energies – with all the uncertainties and unknowns that necessarily constrain such a far-reaching outlook. One example that has recently gained prominence, more than 10 years after Podobnik's article was published is that the boom in unconventional gas (shale gas) and oil production (shale oil, tight oil, oil sands, etc.), especially in North America, "is most clearly identified as a game changer," according to the World Energy Council (Frei 2013: 6). As production volumes of "unconventional" sources continue to increase, "North American energy supply independence" could become "a possibility within less than a decade" (Frei 2013: 6). Such a development was unforeseeable 10 years ago and undermines some of Podobnik's assumptions, even though, at the same time, it illustrates the notion that ironic turns in energy transition processes are a normal aspect of energy transitions. Despite the United States having one of the highest rates of energy consumption in the world, it could become a future energy export nation – which presumably could have far-reaching consequences for global energy prices as well as for government support for renewable energies and entrepreneurial investment in this sector (Mathews 2013: 12). This applies to North America in particular, but it will also affect several other states that are keen to exploit their newly found reservoirs of "unconventionals" or may benefit from decreasing gas or coal prices on the world energy market.[1] According to Frei (2013: 5) the shale gas boom in the United States "has led to a push of discount-priced coal from the US to Europe where it has changed the competitiveness of the companies who took advantage of the changing dynamics."

TRANSITION THEORY AND THE VIRTUES OF EXPERIMENTATION

Since the 1990s, an approach adopted in the field of transition theory has gained increasing attention. Rather than focusing on the long waves of global transitions or on designing future scenarios, it is especially interested in the mechanisms and processes of profound change that occur at the sectoral level of sociotechnical systems, or regimes. This approach has been widely discussed under the heading of a multilevel perspective and applied to several historical studies (e.g. the transition in shipping from sailing ships to steamships;

Geels 2005, Geels and Schot 2010). However, the main issue raised in this approach has to do with the ways sociotechnical change is intertwined with current forms of societal crisis, for example, ecological crises, food crises, and economic crises (Grin *et al.* 2010), and with what form of governance sectoral transitions might be actively managed and steered towards, for example, greater sustainability (see Grin *et al.* 2010, Smith *et al.* 2010). One of the main issues to which the multilevel perspective has been applied is the transformation of (national) energy supply systems, especially the supply of electricity. A number of recent energy transition studies have been presented by Dutch social scientists (Rotmans and Loorbach 2010, Verbong and Geels 2007). These studies were motivated not least by the fact that, for several years now, the Dutch government has given support for official programs and activities relating to "transition management." In 2001, as an integral part of these activities, the Dutch Ministry of Economic Affairs "started developing transition management to accelerate and direct a transition of the Dutch energy supply system. This process has been labeled the energy transition [...] and is an example of a coordinated attempt to accelerate and direct a transition at a national level" (Rotmans and Loorbach 2010: 180). The study by Rotmans and Loorbach (2010) in particular examines the practical achievements, outcomes, and limitations of energy transition management in the Netherlands, although the authors also emphasize the ambitious nature of the goals pursued by the Dutch government:

> The energy transition, as the process of societal change from a fossil-based to a sustainable energy supply system, might be the most complex, long-term transition in any society. It is interwoven with economic sectors (mobility, housing, agriculture) and in fact deeply rooted in our societal structures, routines and culture.
>
> (Rotmans and Loorbach 2010: 196)

The real-life complexity of sociotechnical transitions, as stated here with regard to the energy sector, requires an adequate analytical framework by which transitions can be examined appropriately from a sociological point of view. The multilevel approach has been devised by its protagonists to accomplish this task. What are the main characteristics of this approach? Following Grin *et al.* (2010: 4f.), who sum up the "overarching concepts" of transition analysis, the multilevel perspective:

> conceives of a transition as interference of processes at three levels: innovative practices (niche experiments), structure (the regime), and long-term exogenous trends (the landscape). [...] They represent functional relationships between actors and working practices that are closely interwoven. [...] Only when these different dynamics come together in particular ways may a mutual reinforcement effect emerge as a necessary condition for achieving a transition.
>
> (Grin *et al.* 2010: 4)

This statement (or definition) illustrates that co-evolution is another core element of the multilevel approach (and of transition theory in general as discussed here):

> We speak of co-evolution if the interaction between societal subsystems influences the dynamics of the individual societal subsystems, leading to irreversible patterns of change (...). Economic, cultural, technological, ecological and institutional subsystems co-evolve in many ways and can reinforce each other to co-determine a transition.
>
> (Grin *et al.* 2010: 4)

Furthermore, transition is conceived as a multiphase concept because it describes a transition in time as a sequence of four alternating phases: (1) a pre-development phase, (2) a take-off phase, (3) the acceleration phase, and (4) a stabilization phase (Grin *et al.* 2010). Last but not least, transition theory comprises the concept of co-design and learning:

> This means that knowledge is developed in a complex, interactive design process with a range of stakeholders involved through a process of social learning (...). The underlying rationale is that a synthesis can take place only through frequent interactions between theoretical knowledge, practical knowledge and practical experience, as a result of which innovation can penetrate and take root at the societal system level.
>
> (Grin *et al.* 2010: 5)

Geels and Schot, and Verbong and Loorbach, who have elaborated extensively on the "multilevel perspective on transitions" and have contributed several publications on this issue (e.g. Geels 2002, Geels 2005, Geels and Schot 2007, Geels and Schot 2010, Schot and Geels 2008, Verbong and Loorbach 2012), stress that their approach draws upon a broad multitheoretical background and strives to combine the mutual strengths of two key complementary theoretical approaches, namely science and technology studies (STS) on the one hand and evolutionary economics on the other. The former is oriented towards agency and accommodates sensitivities about micro-processes (such as the social construction of technology approach), while the latter addresses "important broader patterns, such as the emergence of new species (speciation), lineages and trajectories, adaptation in response to changing selection pressures, invasion of new species, extinction." Furthermore, "evolutionary economics developed the concept of technological regime [...]. This regime notion, which captures the structural embeddedness of actors, provides a useful antidote to STS's voluntarist tendencies" (Geels and Schot 2010: 35). Finally, "structuration theory and neo-institutional theory offer insights that complement STS and evolutionary economics," for example, with regard to the embeddedness of agency and structure, the multidimensional characteristics of sociotechnical regimes, the social mechanisms in agency-structure interaction, and the sociological explanation of (sociotechnical) trajectories (Geels and Schot 2010: 42–53).

As mentioned, one of the key issues of transition theory discussed here is the relationship *between* the different levels of analysis: the niche level, the regime level, and the landscape level of macrosocial and macroeconomic structures and developments (or megatrends). These relationships may find expression within various patterns of interaction, whereas Geels and Schot (2010: 27) place their emphasis squarely on the special relationship between niche innovations and the regime level: "The core problem in transitions is not the emergence and development of novelties but their relationship with the existing regime." They continue: "Technological niches and sociotechnical regimes are similar kinds of structures, although different in size and stability." In comparison to niches and regimes, sociotechnical landscapes can be understood as "a different kind of structure. While niches and regimes work through sociological structuration, sociotechnical landscapes influence action differently. [They] do not determine, but provide deep-structural gradients of force that make some actions easier than others" (Geels and Schot 2010: 27–8). In fact, these "deep-structural gradients of force" can affect the relationship between niche innovations and the regime level profoundly. For instance, the remarkable expansion of renewable energy niches in several European countries is due in no small part to "landscape pressure" (Geels and Schot 2007) – especially the emergence of a wide ranging public discourse on the environmental and health risks of nuclear power and fossil energy sources and, not least, the emergence of social movements actively seeking to implement and disseminate alternative energy sources. In some countries, these developments at the macrosocial level are leading to profound changes in public opinion regarding conventional energy technologies and their largely unpredictable consequences. Growing support in society for renewable energy technologies along with a destabilization of incumbent regime structures (e.g. tensions internal to regimes and/or misalignment with new societal and economic challenges) may result. If this occurs, so-called windows of opportunity may open up that support a breakthrough for radical innovations in mass markets, attended by more or less profound changes at the regime level, for example, the *integration* of new energy technologies into the existing regime structure, or the long-lasting and far-reaching *reconfiguration* of the energy supply regime, or even the complete *substitution* of old with new technologies.

In a similar vein, Grin *et al.* (2010), as well as Rotmans and Loorbach (2010), emphasize the analytical relevance of interaction that takes place in between the niche and regime level. By introducing an additional category, the niche-regime level, Grin *et al.* (2010) distinguish several basic patterns of interaction, for example, "a niche to niche-regime pattern, where niches emerge, cluster and form a niche regime which starts to undermine the incumbent regime." Furthermore, they detect a "niche-regime to regime pattern, in which the niche is absorbed or combined with the incumbent regime, which thus evolves into a new regime" (Grin *et al.* 2010: 327). Some observers of transition management (e.g. Hoogma *et al.* 2002, Kemp *et al.* 1998) argue that niches should be understood in beneficial terms as spaces where learning becomes possible through real-world experiments conducted at the local level. The idea is that the uncertainties routinely encountered at the early stages of developing a technology can be reduced by testing it variously within the secure confines of a "quasi-laboratory" (the niche) before it is released to the regime level. However, given the unavoidable uncertainties and unknowns at all three levels of energy transition, we suggest that experimentation is not a characteristic of the niche level alone (which would suggest that experimentation is a factor only in the early stages of development), but rather that the experimental aspects of the energy transition can be found at all three analytical levels. Sociotechnical landscapes may indeed provide deep-structural gradients of force by allowing certain novel possibilities for, say, the diffusion of environmental technologies. However, they do not offer any secure frameworks (legal, economic, cultural) for handling knowledge gaps and unforeseen risks, so that even here various traits of real-world experimentation (see Gross 2003, Gross and Hoffmann-Riem 2005) can be found. These are experiments that take place outside the traditional locales of science and, by so doing, both affect and are affected by seemingly non-scientific elements, such as stakeholder interests, landscape pressures, economic conditions, or the aesthetic preferences of concerned citizens. Experimentation outside niches thus makes it possible to focus precisely on the processes of modeling knowledge at all three levels in order to better understand successes and failures in all fields of the energy transition process (see Chapters 4–8).

SOCIOTECHNICAL TRANSITION PATHWAYS: INTERNAL AND EXTERNAL CAUSES

Alongside these rather theoretical considerations, it may be helpful to present an empirical case of a (national) energy transition in order to illustrate the specific manifestations of niche-regime interactions. For this purpose, we choose the German case because it is characterized by an incumbent power supply regime that, since at least the 1980s, has witnessed the continuing expansion of a renewable energy niche as well as growing landscape pressure. The latter has been due largely to public opinion becoming increasingly critical about the risks posed by nuclear power plants and the pollution emitted by coal-fired power stations (Mautz 2007, Mautz et al. 2008).

The relation between the renewable energy sector and the traditional German electricity system betrays a certain ambiguity. From the very beginning in the 1980s, German protagonists of renewable energies were striving to achieve a paradigm shift in which the centralized system of electricity production, which relied on fossil and nuclear energy sources, was to be replaced with something different. However, from the perspective of the traditional electricity supply regime and its main actors, the new electricity producers constituted an alien force that they initially perceived as an external threat. "Old" and "new" electricity producers faced each other as opponents, separated by a gulf that not only had to do with energy policy but was also ideological, economic, and sociocultural. From the early stages onwards, however, it was necessary to attend to the practical problem of how to link up renewable energy sources reliably and sustainably with the existing electric power grid. As far back as the 1980s, the pioneers of renewable electricity production had, for reasons of practicability, decided against the "radical island" solution of supplying themselves with electricity but had opted instead for a feed-in system in which their self-produced power would be channeled into the national power grid. This strategy corresponded with the emerging design of state funding for renewable energies, which foresaw the provision of state subsidies for the feed-in of electricity into the power grid. The political decision in favor of linking up with renewable energies was one of the preconditions for the subsequent growth of the renewable energy sector, and at the same time, it constituted the starting point of a development that was to alter substantially the perception of an *externally* generated challenge.

Over the years it has been possible, to a large extent, for the established electricity sector to internalize the innovative ideas and practices prompted by the upsurge of renewable energies without losing their dynamic potential for change in the process. After a long period of resistance, all the major German power companies are now involved in the process of expanding renewable power generation. They took this step in order to influence the future direction of development in the renewable energy sector. In keeping with their traditional business model of centralized power generation, the investment plans drawn up so far by the large electric power companies focus mainly on developing huge offshore wind farms in both domestic and foreign waters.

Unlike the incumbent electricity supply regime, the German renewable energy sector enjoys broad support within civil society. Thus, it remains capable of sending powerful messages to the political and legislative authorities regarding energy policy, including, for example, demands for a thoroughgoing decentralization of electricity generation, a process of restructuring in line with environmentally sound principles, and calls to overhaul oligopolistic market structures in the energy sector. At the same time, a growing number of small and medium enterprises (SME) in the industry have been pressing ahead with the expansion of renewable energies. In the course of this expansion, the renewable energy sector has become an *intra-system component* that, because of its technical requirements, has prompted a range of restructuring measures within the overall system architecture. This is important given that it is only by integrating renewable energy – with its partial dependency on the weather – into the power supply system in an efficient way that its economic and environmental potential can be properly harnessed. The challenges facing the old as well as the new power companies in the German electricity generating system have been growing for several years now. One of their key tasks is to contribute actively towards ensuring the stability and safety of the grid and the power supply, in part by means of incremental steps towards restructuring. This shared commitment to system security has become a driving force for the internalization of what was originally perceived to be an external challenge to the system.

These developments are significant – not least from the perspective of sociological analysis – because they point to the fact that the changes occurring within the German electricity sector due to the expansion of renewable energy facilities can no longer be adequately interpreted as a clash between internal forces of stabilization and external forces of radical change, as was the case during the pioneering phase of renewable electricity.

Recent sociological analyses in the field of transition theory, which is concerned with the stabilizing and destabilizing factors affecting sociotechnical systems, have similarly rejected the notion of a polarization between internal forces of continuity and external triggers of (radical) system change in favor of a stronger emphasis on the interaction between niche dynamics and developments at the level of sociotechnical regimes. Thus, Schot and Geels (2008: 547) conclude that "niche innovations (…) need not always compete with and substitute the prevailing regime, as was assumed in earlier SNM (strategic niche management) work. They may also be incorporated and transform the regime from within." According to them, what we are dealing with, as shown by the German case, are specific patterns of co-evolution in which "the dynamic is less about substitution and more about how niches can branch, pile up, and contribute to changes in the behaviour, practices and routines of existing regime actors." In a nutshell, therefore, their analysis constitutes "a more differentiated view of niche-regime interaction" (Schot and Geels 2008: 547).

In their investigation of the conditions of sectoral change, Dolata and Werle (2007: 34–35) argue in a similar vein. According to them, the use of "dichotomous typifications," which distinguish only between long periods of stability and rare incidents of radical upheaval triggered by "exogenous shocks," turns out to be an inappropriate tool for analysis. Much more typical are "gradual transformations" through processes of incremental restructuring and adaptation. As a consequence of cumulative effects, such processes may well lead to "entirely new system architectures" and therefore to a similarly strong pressure for change, as is more commonly associated with external shocks. Moreover, because of the pressure for innovation exerted by "new cross-over technologies" (e.g. microelectronics, new information technologies), a technological "lock-in" of entire sectors is less likely today than it was in earlier phases of sociotechnical development. Such a process of gradual transformation can hardly be attributed to forces that are unambiguously external or internal to the system. It is much more plausible to assume an interplay of endogenous processes that are prompted and advanced by actors from within the system as well as by new external actors forcing their way into the system with different ideas and practices (see Dolata 2013). Such a transition, distinguished by interaction rather than by polarity, appears to be characteristic of the German electricity sector in its current form (as in 2014). Here, in fact, a number of different forms of system restructuring are in competition with each other – their various combinations contain strategic elements of both system integration and system change in relation to renewable energies. In any event, they are poorly served by the analytical dichotomy "incremental change versus radical transformation."

The notion of transition is not only of theoretical interest but also entails practical implications in various policy fields. As mentioned previously, a key aspect of the transition approach is the desire to bring about positive change in society (or in societal subsystems). In this context, the majority of studies focus on transitions towards sustainable development (e.g. Geels 2010, Grin *et al.* 2010, Jacobsson and Lauber 2006, Kemp *et al.* 1998, Podobnik 2006, Raven 2007, Schneidewind and Augenstein 2012, Smith *et al.* 2010). A major topic addressed by several of these studies is the emergence – or deliberate development – of a governance concept that is properly suited to achieve the objectives of sustainability in different societal domains, for example, energy supply, farming, or motorized personal transport. Grin *et al.* (2010) discuss two Dutch governance concepts known as strategic niche management (SNM) and transition management (TM). From their point of view, the core task of "transition governance in any form" is to build "connections between innovative practice experiments," which occur in sociotechnical niches, and "changes at the regime level" (Grin *et al.* 2010: 334). In a quite similar way, Smith *et al.* (2010) distinguish between existing regimes as "a de facto form of governance in the sense that they structure and order the interaction *of* material artifacts and social processes" on the one hand and "purposeful governance for sustainable development" on the other, which requires an "analysis *for* deliberate policy aiming to transform regimes" (Smith *et al.* 2010: 444). Here too, the niche-regime relationship is looked upon as one of the key elements of the transition approach. In this context, it is important to consider the societal distribution of structural power – and the inequalities of this distribution – that helps (or hinders) the advent of significant sociotechnical change. Smith *et al.* (2010) emphasize the fact that structural power is not necessarily the reserve of members of the incumbent regime. Instead, structural power may emerge from "resources in actor networks beyond the regime," for example, from niche actors who are able to communicate "knowledge about alternatives" to the public, or from social movements that call into question traditional "legitimacy issues" (Smith *et al.* 2010: 445). As shown earlier, the activities engaged in by German civil society to promote renewable energies are a good example of this kind of growing structural power aimed at bringing about a purposeful transformation of the incumbent electricity regime (see Mautz 2007). Thus, "power relations alter" because "new discourses generate new expectations about the adequacy of regime performance, such as its sustainability, and contribute to a re-ordering of priorities" (Smith *et al.* 2010: 445). All in all, the emergence and shaping of sustainability governance must be seen as a deliberate sociopolitical process involving a diverse array of – often antagonistic – actor groups and innovation networks (see Kowol and Küppers 2005). These observations raise a number of questions for further research, whose purpose must be not only "to improve our understanding of niches, in terms of their development and their wider influence" (Smith *et al.* 2010: 445), but also to continue to examine the processes, mechanisms, and causes of regime destabilization: "how do regimes open up, erode or decline?" (Smith *et al.* 2010: 445). This in turn raises questions about "the interests and sources of power-shaping selection environments and generating variations" and about "coalition formation around different niches and lobbies for different kinds of sociotechnical transitions" (Smith *et al.* 2010: 446). Transition theory therefore pursues ambitious goals in the field of sustainability – a fact that Grin *et al.* (2010: 322f.) highlight as they underscore the radical nature of their own approach: "The transitions approach goes beyond the idea of win–win, new business opportunities, competitive advantage, people, planet and profit (central to many expressions of ecological modernization and also sustainable development approaches) and acknowledges that we have to face deeper changes and hard choices."

Furthermore, many relevant empirical studies in environmental sociology, STS, and the sociology of science are united in calling for a better understanding of energy transitions and the multilevel perspective, especially with regard to so-called breakthroughs, that is, the points at which technological innovations manage to overcome the social, cultural, and economic barriers represented by an existing regime (see Hess 2012, Vasi 2010, Verbong and Loorbach 2012). In seeking to respond to this call, we examine in the remainder of this book some of the key aspects of transition management.

NOTE

1 As Frei (2013: 6) states, there are projects "being developed around the world which will eventually change the global supply map."

4

WIND, SOLAR, AND BIOMASS IN SOCIOTECHNICAL TRANSITION

This chapter is based on the key assumption that the expansion of renewable energies all over the world is not only the result of technical innovations and positive practical experiences but also an outcome of specific processes of cultural and institutional renewal, including the role of non-governmental organizations (NGOs) and special interest groups. However, unlike in the 1980s and 1990s, sociologists nowadays pay relatively scant attention to the environmental movement (activists, organizations, and institutions). This is especially true when it comes to one of the most pressing issues of our time, namely how to satisfy the growing energy needs of societies in virtually every corner of the world. In this regard, Hein-Anton van der Heijden (2010) has pointed out some of the ways in which social movements can actually influence policy processes relating to energy generation, including participation in policy committees and raising the public's awareness of relevant issues. Focusing on the wind energy sector as an example, Ion Bogdan Vasi (2010) has argued that the development of wind energy is dependent not only on improvements in technology and on economic factors but, first and foremost, on the efforts of the environmental movement. Vasi shows how the environmental movement has been an important driver of market formation and industrial growth in the wind energy sector, working through various industry and policy channels. Unlike many social movement researchers who have analyzed opportunity structures, advocacy groups, and influences on organizational change via protests or boycotts, Vasi focuses on the impact that the environmental movement has had on the emerging wind energy industry. In Vasi's comparison of several countries with similar wind power potential, Denmark and Germany stand out as particularly strong in the wind energy sector because the environmental movement also has a strong voice there. Vasi describes the adoption strategies deployed in pro-wind energy policies, including renewable energy feed-in tariffs in Denmark, Germany, and Spain and renewable portfolio standards in North America and the United Kingdom. Finally, Vasi shows that over the last 40 years the US environmental movement appears to have had little impact on federal energy policies but has been able nonetheless to contribute significantly to localized demand for renewable energy. This can be exemplified by the decision of many universities in the United States to purchase renewable energy certificates (especially from wind energy sources), accounting for "over 3.1 GW of new renewable energy capacity additions" (Vasi 2010: 140) within a single decade. In sum, the environmental movement may have been able to affect market formation by fostering the adoption of specific environmental policies on the one hand and influencing consumers' perceptions in order to stimulate demand for new energy products on the other. This in turn may also have led to changes in attitude within traditional industrial sectors towards more renewable energy generation.

Although the environmental movement is crucial to our understanding of global transitions towards renewable energy sources, there are many more issues to be taken into account when trying to get a clearer picture of the different types of energy transitions taking place all over the world. To do so, the following chapters examine further reasons for the increasing diffusion of renewable energies worldwide by pointing to the relevance of political regulation, social movements, and stakeholder networks that have played an important role in the process of innovation.

THE RISE OF RENEWABLE ENERGIES

The electricity sector in many European countries, in North America and, increasingly, in a number of Asian countries has been shaped significantly by two distinctive features. The first of these is what might be called a "traditional path," characterized by certain technical and economic structures that emerged at the beginning of the twentieth century and have remained substantially the same to this day. Up until now, the dominant paradigm has been one of centralized generation and distribution of electricity within a large interlocking technical system (Hughes 1987, Markard and Truffer 2006) based for the most part on large-scale coal-fired and nuclear power plants (Podobnik 2006). Alongside this technical setup, market concentration is a characteristic feature of the electricity sector in countries as varied as Germany, the United States, France, and Spain. An oligopoly of a few energy suppliers has traditionally dominated the production and distribution of power. In spite of sporadic "interruptions" to this traditional energy pathway, its continuity has in most cases remained constant. Neither the oil crisis of the 1970s, the "limits to growth" debate that followed it, nor even critical debates around nuclear power and environmental protection triggered a rupture in or even a withdrawal from centralized power generation on the basis of fossil and nuclear energy resources. Indeed, paradoxically, the liberalization of the German electricity market, which began in 1998 with the Energy Industry Act, even stabilized the process of economic concentration. In Germany, four suppliers came to dominate the electricity market and are still responsible for about 70 percent of the country's entire electricity production (as of 2013).[1] Considering their economic dominance, organizational structures, and long-term investment strategies, there is considerable evidence to indicate that the major companies in the electricity sector will continue to pursue their well-trodden path in the future. This assumption has been confirmed by recent announcements in Germany concerning investments in new lignite and hard coal power plants (see Morris 2012), as well as by French and British plans to invest in nuclear energy, not to mention the investments in new nuclear power plants in India and China (see www.world-nuclear.org). All this suggests that the road towards change will be a long and slow one. As of 2014, mainland China has 17 nuclear reactors in operation, 28 under construction, and many more in the planning process. The urgency expressed in much energy transition rhetoric – especially since the Fukushima disaster in 2011 – sometimes makes it easy to forget that, based on past experience, energy shifts are inherently slow and incremental processes.

The second distinctive feature of the European electricity sector is structural change and innovation, a prevalent perception based on the success story of the European renewable energy sector. Here, Germany – alongside Denmark and Spain – is perceived as playing an internationally recognized pioneering role, namely as the world market leader in the field of wind energy (Vasi 2010) and as a major international producer of other types of renewable energy technologies such as photovoltaic cells that convert energy from the sun directly into electricity (Grau *et al.* 2012). The business strategies of energy companies – especially those of wind turbine and solar cell manufacturers – are largely focused on international markets nowadays. Germany in particular has become "a lead market for renewables and a leader in technology and innovation in several fields" (BMU 2005: 9). In 2013, the renewable energy sector accounted for around 23.5 percent of total power generation in Germany (BMU 2013a: 5). It can therefore no longer be judged as economically insignificant. With a total turnover of 34.3 billion Euros in 2012 (BMU 2013a: 30–31) and having secured "significantly more" jobs (about 378,000 in 2012) than "coal-fired and nuclear power plants combined" (BMU 2005: 4, 2013a: 32), it has become an expanding sector of the economy.

However, the German case must be seen as part of an overall global trend in which renewable energies account for an increasing share of final energy consumption. From the early years of the present millennium, two technologies have seen particularly rapid growth: photovoltaic and wind energy.

The basis of what has come to be known as the photovoltaic effect was discovered as far back as 1839 by Alexandre Edmond Becquerel.

Becquerel observed that when exposed to light the voltage, or electric current, in different materials increases. Although Albert Einstein was awarded the 1921 Nobel Prize in Physics for explaining in 1905 the mechanism underlying this observation (the photoelectric effect), it was only in 1954 that the first working photovoltaic cell was developed. At the time, it converted some 0.5 percent of incoming sunlight into electricity. In the following two decades, the efficiency of solar cells was improved, but it was only in the 1970s that the cost of photovoltaic cells went down considerably, enabling the commercialization of applications ranging from traffic signs to lighthouses. Beginning with the founding of the Solar Energy Research Institute in Colorado, United States, major research programs in most Western countries led to further improvements in the cost and efficiency of photovoltaic cells, which by the 1980s became sources of electricity for everyday electronic devices (see Perlin 1999). Countries such as Japan and Germany set up subsidy programs from the early 1990s in order to promote improvements in photovoltaic cells. The installed capacity of photovoltaic panels in the EU member states saw considerable expansion between 2000 and 2011, from 180 megawatt-peak (MW_p) to about 68 gigawatt-peak (GW_p) (BMU 2012: 69, 2013a: 69).

The utilization of wind power has a considerably longer history than that of photovoltaic cells. The first pioneering efforts at generating electricity by windmills were successful as early as the late nineteenth century (see later). The manufacturing and distribution of modern wind turbines began in Denmark and the United States during the 1970s and gradually spread widely throughout most European countries from the 1990s onwards. Like photovoltaic cells, the dissemination of wind turbines accelerated from 2000 onwards and installed capacity in the EU increased from 12,732 MW in 2000 to 105,696 MW in 2012 (BMU 2013a: 65). On closer inspection, however, marked differences become apparent between the different EU member states. For instance, the photovoltaic boom of the previous decade was sustained mainly by Germany, Spain, and Italy. The expansion of power generation by wind turbines has taken place mainly in seven EU member states so far: Germany, Spain, United Kingdom, France, Italy, Denmark, and Portugal (albeit with marked differences between them). However, the main source of renewable energy within the EU is still electricity from large hydropower plants, a traditional source of electricity in most member states. In twelve EU member states, hydropower is the leading renewable source of electricity, contributing some 46 percent to the total amount of renewable power consumption in the EU in 2011 (306.1 TeraWatt hours (TWh) out of a total 670.6 TWh, see Table 4.1). Thus, in relation to total power consumption in the EU in 2011 (3,280 TWh), hydropower accounted for 9.3 percent, whereas all "new" renewable energy technologies together (wind power, photovoltaic, geothermal plants, modern biomass, and biogas plants) accounted for 11.1 percent, meaning that renewables made an overall contribution to power consumption of 20.4 percent (see Figure 4.1, BMU 2013a: 60–1).

At the global level there is an even greater disparity between countries and regions regarding the generation of renewable energies. In addition to a number of EU member states, as shown above, a few other countries have entered the major international league of renewable energy investors, with China and the United States ranked first and second and Japan, India, and Brazil among the top ten in 2012 (BMU 2013a: 84, see Table 4.2).

On the other hand there are large regions – and even whole continents – of the world where "new" renewable energies still play only a very marginal role. In Africa, renewable energies are generated almost entirely by traditional biomass (accounting for 96.9 percent of total renewables used in 2010), and solid biomass is the dominant renewable energy source in Asia/Oceania (accounting for 79.3 percent of total renewables used in 2010; hydropower: 13.5 percent). In Latin America, the use of renewable energies is also based mainly on traditional biomass (65.5 percent in 2010) and on a comparatively large proportion of hydropower (32.6 percent in 2010) (BMU 2013a: 80).

Even in China – now a frontrunner regarding investment in "new" renewable energies – traditional biomass is still the main source of renewable energy (with 76.0 percent of total renewables use in 2009) alongside large hydropower plants (BMU 2012: 96). This is no coincidence given that biomass is a generic category that covers all biologically produced matter. However, it is still wood that accounts for the largest proportion of all biomass energy sources because biomass power

Table 4.1 Electricity supply from renewables in the EU 27 in 2011

	Hydro-power	Wind energy	Biomass	Biogenic fraction of waste (TWh)	Photo-voltaic	Geothermal energy	Total	Renewables' share of gross electricity consumption (%)
Austria	34.2	1.9	4.3	0.2	0.2	–	40.8	55.2
Belgium	0.2	2.3	3.9	0.8	1.2	–	8.4	9.0
Bulgaria	2.9	0.9	0.1	–	0.1	–	3.9	9.8
Cyprus	–	0.1	–	–	0.01	–	0.13	2.5
Czech Republic	2.0	0.4	2.6	0.1	2.2	–	7.2	10.3
Denmark	0.02	9.8	3.4	1.0	0.02	–	14.2	38.8
Estonia	0.03	0.4	0.8	–	–	–	1.2	12.6
Finland	12.4	0.5	11.0	0.3	0.01	–	24.2	27.7
France	44.8	12.2	2.9	2.2	2.1	0.2	65.0[a]	12.8
Germany	17.3	48.9	32.8	4.8	19.3	–	123.1	20.3
Greece	4.0	3.3	0.2	–	0.6	–	8.1	13.0
Hungary	0.2	0.6	1.7	–	0.001	–	2.7	6.4
Ireland	0.7	4.4	0.3	0.1	–	–	5.4	19.4
Italy	45.2	9.9	8.6	2.2	10.8	5.7	82.3	23.6
Latvia	2.9	0.1	0.12	–	–	–	3.1	41.9
Lithuania	0.5	0.5	0.2	–	–	–	1.1	9.6
Luxemburg	0.1	0.1	0.1	0.04	0.03	–	0.2	3.0
Malta	–	–	–	–	–	–	–	–

(Continued)

Table 4.1 Continued

	Hydro-power	Wind energy	Biomass	Biogenic fraction of waste (TWh)	Photo-voltaic	Geothermal energy	Total	Renewables' share of gross electricity consumption (%)
Netherlands	0.1	5.1	5.0	2.0	0.1	–	12.3	10.1
Poland	2.3	3.2	7.6	–	–	–	13.1	8.3
Portugal	11.5	9.2	2.6	0.3	0.3	0.2	24.1	43.6
Romania	14.7	1.4	0.2	–	0.001	–	16.3	27.1
Slovakia	3.8	0.01	0.8	0.02	0.4	–	5.0	17.0
Slovenia	3.6	–	0.3	–	0.1	–	3.9	26.2
Spain	30.6	42.4	3.8	0.7	7.4	–	86.2[b]	30.2
Sweden	66.4	6.1	9.7	1.9	0.01	–	84.1	58.7
United Kingdom	5.7	15.5	11.2	1.7	0.3	–	34.4	9.2
EU 27	306.1	179.0	114.2	18.3	45.0	6.1	670.6	20.4

Source: BMU (2013a: 61).

Notes:
[a]Total includes 0.5 TWh generated by the tidal power plant "La Rance".
[b]Total includes 1.3 TWh generated by concentrated thermal solar power plants.

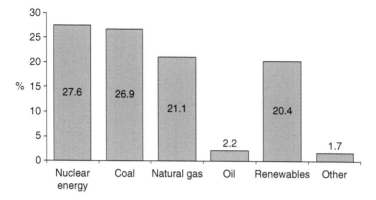

Figure 4.1 Structure of total electricity supply in the EU 27 in 2011.
Source: BMU (2013a: 60).

Table 4.2 National investment in the renewable energy sector[a]

	2011 (billion US$)	*2012 (billion US$)*
China	54.1	65.1
United States	56.8	35.6
Germany	31.3	22.8
Rest of EU 27	17.7	16.3
Japan	9.3	16.3
Italy	30.1	14.7
United Kingdom	10.0	8.3
India	12.5	6.9
South Africa		5.5
Brazil	7.8	5.3

Source: BMU (2013a: 84).

Notes:
[a]Excluding public and private investment in research and development.

plants mainly use wood as a fuel.[2] Furthermore, the distribution of biomass products requires novel forms of collaboration and management across different industries and policy sectors in order to meet local and regional demand for food, fuel, and fiber (see Sauter *et al.*

2013). The availability of land for biomass production is a major issue and a primary constraint in the development of bio-economy sectors all over the world due to conflicts over land use for different purposes (see Rathmann *et al.* 2010). In all countries involved in transitioning towards renewable energy utilization, the transformation towards a bio-economy is still in its early stages. New technologies and infrastructure designs are in their infancy and there is often scant knowledge regarding criteria for evaluating sustainability or measures for ensuring the efficiency of emerging value chains based on the use of biomass resources (see Szarka *et al.* 2013).

Although the sustainable and sufficient supply of biomass currently plays an important role in the transformation of fossil fuel-based economies, biomass is also a limited resource and has to satisfy different societal demands. The growing demand for biomass increases the pressure on land, inducing unforeseen changes in land use. Furthermore, the intensification of biomass production can result in nutrient deficiency in soils and a loss of habitat and biodiversity. In addition to the biomass issue, the current ambiguity apparent in the Chinese energy transition also finds expression in the fact that China is not only expanding its nuclear power supply (see earlier) but will also continue to depend heavily on coal-fired power plants over the coming decades. New coal-fired power plants, each with a capacity of about 900 MW, are currently being connected to the country's electricity grid every week (Fücks 2013: 56). At the same time, within just a few years China has built up the world's largest capacity of wind power, with a nominal capacity of 75,564 MW in 2012 (BMU 2013a: 65). Thus, in a study on "the greening of capitalism," Mathews (2013: 9) speaks of "the 'green and black' paradox of China": it "is now burning nearly as much coal as the rest of the world combined," and yet at the same time, "China's green investments are already matching its 'black' investments in fossil-fuelled energy systems" (Mathews 2013: 7). According to Mathews' – optimistic – point of view, the paradox could be resolved in the near future because "green development is emerging as the 'inevitable choice' for China" due to growing energy insecurity, devastating health problems caused by pollution, and a national government "that is prepared to act" (Mathews 2013: 7).

To sum up, the traditional energy sources, solid biomass (mostly wood) and hydropower, continue to dominate the worldwide use of renewable energies. In 2010, renewable energies constituted 16.9 percent of global final energy consumption, 15.4 percent of this consisted of solid biomass and hydropower and just 1.5 percent was "new" renewable energy technologies (see Figure 4.2, Figure 4.3).

As global energy consumption and renewable energy generation saw nearly the same rate of growth between 2000 and 2010, the contribution of renewables to the total global energy supply increased

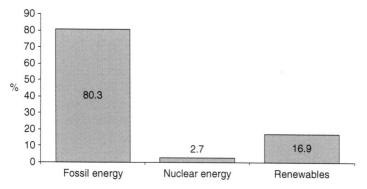

Figure 4.2 Global final energy consumption in 2010.
Source: BMU (2013a: 76).

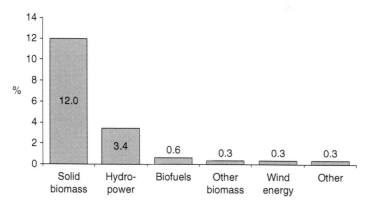

Figure 4.3 Global final energy consumption in 2010: renewables only.
Source: BMU (2013a: 76).

only marginally during that period (BMU 2013a: 79). This fact highlights a serious problem concerning any future energy transition: given that the exploitation of "traditional" renewable energies is reaching its limits "and in some cases cannot be classified as sustainable use of renewable energy sources" (BMU 2013a: 77), any future expansion of renewable energies in favor of climate protection and sustainability will have to be based mainly on the previously mentioned "new" technologies in this field. However, this will require an accelerated dynamic in the renewables sector. The future challenge is to offset the increase in global energy consumption by achieving sufficient global growth rates in renewable energy production using modern technologies.

In the following section, we offer some insights regarding the sociotechnical dynamics that have so far been the driving force behind renewables, development in some pioneering countries, and could possibly set an example for further global dissemination of these technologies.

RENEWABLE ENERGIES AS EXPERIMENTS IN INNOVATION

If we think of renewable energies as a radical form of innovation as opposed to an incremental one (see Braun-Thürmann 2005, Dolata 2013, Werle 2012), it is worth bearing in mind at the same time that biomass, water power, wind energy, and, in some areas, even geothermal energy constituted the basic energy sources of pre-modern societies and that most of the modern technologies that are used to harness renewable energy sources were invented several decades before the 1970s. Hence from a technological point of view, it seems inappropriate to describe renewable energies as radical innovations. Perhaps a more apt conception would accord with David Edgerton's thesis that not only do most inventions take place in the world of use but, in particular, the importance of the "old" for contemporary social change is often much greater than expected. In addition, major change "is taking place by the transfer of techniques from place to place" (Edgerton 2007: 209). This latter phenomenon can be viewed in the context of sociological research on so-called immutable mobiles, a term originally introduced by Bruno Latour (1987) to refer to technologies that retain their overall shape but are moved and experimentally shaped to fit other contexts (see Akrich 1993, de Laet and Mol 2000, Eglash *et al.* 2004). Perhaps, therefore, the process of innovation towards renewable energy utilization ought rather to be conceptualized as one of rediscovering and further developing the previously mentioned technologies as part of an overall evolutionary process of advancement. The learning entailed by such a process is based on a series of small experimental steps, embedded in new social contexts, and linked to wider societal and environmental objectives. After all, the use of renewable energy from windmills, for example, is almost as old as human civilization itself. The earliest records indicating the existence of knowledge about how to use wind power are found in the context of plans for an irrigation project in Babylonia in the seventeenth century BC and, albeit much later, in Persian designs dated around 200 BC. The use of windmills as devices for grinding grain is recorded first in France in 1105 and in England in 1180. From then, they spread all over Europe and then worldwide (see Sathyajith 2006: 2–4). According to Matthias Heymann's (1995) historical reconstruction, there were more than 200,000 windmills in Europe by the middle of the nineteenth century. Around the turn of the twentieth century, about 9,000 windmills existed in the Netherlands alone, with some 20,000 in Germany and roughly 2,500 in Denmark. Estimates indicate that between 1850 and 1900, about 6 million small windmills were installed on US farms to operate irrigation pumps. Viewed from this perspective, the world still has a long way to go if the number of windmills in existence in the twenty-first century is to match those that existed in the nineteenth century. With regard to electricity generation, it was Charles Brush who, in 1887, started producing electricity using a wind powered generator, and a few years later Poul la Cour constructed a wind turbine to generate electricity in his home in Denmark (see Heymann 1995, Sathyajith 2006: 5). Today both small-scale wind power facilities at household and community level, as well as large groups of turbines (wind farms) are used to produce electricity. The use of windmills on different scales to generate significant quantities of electricity for modern society is a novel phenomenon and, as such, can also be seen as inherently uncertain and therefore experimental. Since windmills work on both the small-scale level of the household in residential areas (see Bovet and Köck 2012), as well as on the large-scale level of industry, there are inevitable uncertainties and knowledge gaps involved that need to be coped with in the future. This applies especially to the question concerning which mode of niche-regime interaction needs to be developed in order to support the systemic integration of an increasing number of decentralized power sources that, in the case of wind turbines (and photovoltaic panels), are characterized by intermittent power generation (see the following and Chapters 7 and 8). Since no blueprints exist for this type of systemic integration, it appears appropriate to conceptualize what is happening in many countries as a venture into the unknown via a process of real-world experimentation.

In the concept of real-world experimentation, conceived originally in the field of science and technology studies (STS), extreme events such as the Chernobyl nuclear accident in 1986 are understood as retrospective experiments (Krohn and Weingart 1987). Similarly, the notion of viewing processes outside the laboratory as experiments goes back to Francis Bacon's reflections on the relationship between the experimental method and society. Bacon was influential in the formation of the world view that distinguishes the realm of the experimenter from that of the objects experimented upon, a view that privileges (rational) human beings as masters over a world to which they essentially do not belong. Much less well known, however, was Bacon's provocative proposition that to grant the experimental method pre-eminence in science would be to turn society itself into a large-scale experiment (see Gross and Krohn 2004). On the basis of this view, modern society should give the experimental method an experimental opportunity because promises of the gains of modern science cannot be justified by anticipatory argument, but only by practicing and implementing the new method in the wider society. Thus, understood, the real-world experiments taking place outside the realm of science are indeed not easily reproducible, controllable, or reversible, and yet it seems reasonable to hypothesize that the laboratory experiment is becoming the exception rather than the rule. Assuming this to be the case, any critical analysis of such real-world experiments would require research on natural processes as well as on novel cultural practices, forms of political participation, societal organization, alternative lifestyles, and innovative technologies. Situating not only processes of energy innovation, but also of exnovation, (the phasing out of technologies and energy utilization practices that hamper a transition towards renewables) within this understanding of experiments makes it possible to render unexpected events as not necessarily straightforwardly negative, but often as crucial in order to learn and help create better and safer technological solutions.

The term "experimenting society" was developed by Donald Campbell (1917–1996) and associates in the 1960s. It amounted to a call for modern society to agree to apply the experimental method to public policy – the public sphere was seen as a suitable place for social scientists to test the efficacy of political programs. Campbell indicated the nature of the experimenting society in this way: "Faced with a choice between innovating a new program or commissioning a thorough study of the problem as a prelude to action, the bias would be toward innovating" (Campbell 1998: 39). For Campbell, however, the responsibilities of reform politics must always rest with the scientists, and thus learning took place first and foremost within the academic community and not – despite what the name implies – in the wider experimental society.

Subsequently, the desire to develop an understanding of experimentation beyond the laboratory walls has been spurred on more generally by the observation that modern research in general has tended to be extended beyond the laboratory walls to test institutional practices and thus assumptions about safety (see Herbold 1995, Weyer 2008). In this kind of scenario, the traditional boundaries between technology development and the production of detached scientific knowledge on the one hand and the application of knowledge and technologies in the wider society on the other become transformed. As of the early 2000s, the idea of the real-world experiment has been developed further as a means of designing socially useful and technically feasible ecological design in situations of uncertainty and knowledge gaps (Gross and Hoffmann-Riem 2005, Gross and Krohn 2004, Gross 2010a). In order to engage meaningfully in such experiments and to cope with nonknowledge and uncertainty, the stakeholders involved – at the niche, regime, and landscape levels – need to be open towards the possibility of redefining goals in the course of iterative discussions. Experiments of this kind are most likely to be conducted in areas where uncertainty appears to be controllable and knowledge gaps are clearly defined. Stefan Böschen (2013) has introduced the notion of "formative publics" to describe networks of actors and institutions that have become part of the controversies surrounding projects involving technological innovation. As such, these publics can be regarded as the social context in which real-world experiments occur, becoming part of the experiment by participating in negotiating the consequences of novel technologies at all three levels of the transition processes and doing so in either a supportive or an obstructive way.

Thus, the early phase of innovation and diffusion of renewable energies in most Western countries was associated largely with the rise of the new social movements – particularly those such as the ecological and the alternative movement – as formative publics in the 1970s. Although there were no radical technological innovations to debate during this early phase, there certainly were new radical – and in part even utopian – ideas and objectives that prompted a reinterpretation of established technologies at the landscape level. This especially applies to Germany where the new social movements and their struggle against nuclear power and pollution from coal-fired power plants attracted considerable attention from the 1970s onwards – from the wider public and from politicians alike. Consequently, seeing Germany's efforts to radically shift its infrastructure towards renewable energy utilization as part of a major European experiment – a testing ground for a transnational European identity as Alfred Nordmann (2009) proposed – is only one interpretation. What this shift also implies is stated in a recent editorial piece published in the scientific journal *Nature*:

> Merkel and the German public are displaying admirable courage in turning the country into a laboratory for energy policies (and technologies) which could become models for many industrialized countries. That the nation is running this costly and risky self-experiment against the background of a European arch financial crisis should stand as an enduring testament to Merkel's leadership.
>
> (*Nature* 2013: 138)

Having focused in this chapter on the conceptual aspects of renewable energy technologies, we are now in a position to underscore the significance of the social shaping of technological innovations (see Pinch and Bijker 1987, Hughes 1987), as well as the importance of collective stakeholders active in this field. It seems clear today that most stakeholders directly involved in the field of renewable energies – citizens groups, local utilities, operators of wind turbines or solar power plants, to name just a few – are seeking to advance a paradigm change in the energy system. The fundamental principles of the new paradigm as we perceive it are:

- decentralizing energy production in technical and economic terms;
- extending and pluralizing the group of those actively involved in the energy sector;
- protecting the environment and combating climate change; and
- phasing out nuclear energy and fossil fuels.

These principles of a new paradigm also apply to a relatively new area of energy utilization, namely the heat found below the Earth's crust. As we have seen, most disciplines dealing with renewable energies and the opportunities and limitations regarding their dissemination, have focused mainly on wind, solar, biomass, and, to a lesser extent, hydropower. Geothermal power, the internal heat stored in the depths of the Earth, has received comparatively scant attention. Whereas renewable energy sources are normally perceived as coming from above the ground, in the next chapter we turn to a renewable energy source from below the ground that has come to the fore in both research and policy circles only in the last few decades: geothermal heat.

NOTES

1 For current data, see www.energieverbraucher.de/de/Konzentration_358/ (accessed June 26, 2013).
2 Only biomass power plants in the pulp and paper industry use fiber sludge and other residues from their production processes instead of wood (see Sauter *et al.* 2013).

5

RENEWABLE ENERGY
FROM BELOW
THE GROUND

Although modern societies are sitting on top of an almost endless renewable resource – geothermal heat – for various reasons very few countries have so far resolved to make use of it. Even Iceland, for example, which has very favorable conditions for tapping geothermal heat, based its energy supply on fossil fuels up until the 1970s. This is all the more surprising given that geothermal heat has been an integral part of human existence from prehistoric times in the form of caves that were warmer than the air temperature outside or thermal wells that were used for heating or washing. During Roman times, particularly from the first century AD onwards, hot springs were used to fill public baths and even to operate heating installations beneath the floors of houses in places such as Bath in the United Kingdom. Perhaps the longest lasting geothermal "district heating system" was started in Chaudes-Aigues in the Auvergne in France sometime in the fourteenth century. It is still working today. However, it was only with the advent of the Renaissance and later of the Enlightenment ideal of science that people began to observe the heat inside the Earth with analytic interest. Inspired by experience from mining operations, which became more and more important at the close of the medieval age, miners observed an increase in heat the deeper they moved underground. It was in 1680 that Robert Boyle discovered that the temperature of the Earth rose progressively the further one probed towards the center. Despite this, up until the first half of the nineteenth century geologists were still unable to agree whether or not the temperature inside the Earth rose towards the center or not. Some theories even claimed that the Earth's interior was hollow and that the temperature was lower the further inside one went. Other theories postulated a host of interconnecting tubes and caves in the interior that were said to give rise to unstable and changing temperatures in different areas (see Dean 1992, Greene 1983, Lesser 1987). However, these debates were settled in the course of the nineteenth century and, in particular, in the early years of the twentieth century when, in 1904, the first power plant to make use of geothermal energy for electric power production was launched in Larderello in Italy by Piero Ginori Conti.

Today's comparative lack of interest in geothermal energy as an alternative energy source, however, may have to do with the fact that tapping geothermal energy has so far been limited to areas near tectonic plate boundaries, such as the Larderello dry steam field in Italy or the many hot wells in Iceland and Hawaii. However, it almost certainly has to do also with the fact that the Earth's heat has not played a prominent role in public debates on clean energy. This is because clean, renewable or sustainable energy is associated in most people's minds with sources above the Earth's surface, whereas what comes from below is widely considered dirty, mysterious, muddy, and dark – and definitely not clean.[1]

THE SPECIFIC POSITION OF GEOTHERMAL ENERGY AS A RENEWABLE ENERGY SOURCE

It appears timely to consider the cultural foundations of subterranean energy given that recent technological developments have expanded the range of its potential applications. These potential uses range from novel ways of heating homes to providing a significant share of the energy mix, especially if heat is tapped from several kilometers below the Earth's surface. Given that many of the recently launched geothermal power plants and associated drilling technologies exhibit many scientific unknowns, questions relating to the unintended side effects of the method (including earthquakes) are of crucial importance. Since this type of energy can be harnessed at both an industrial and a household scale, important new interdisciplinary questions arise regarding the design of the technology and how it relates to existing sociotechnical systems. These questions also highlight the respective political valence of local energy production as opposed to large-scale, corporate production.

Furthermore, the extrusion of lava from volcanoes reminds us in rather dramatic fashion that an enormous amount of heat exists in the Earth's interior. This heat generates pressures that, in some cases, are manifested only a few kilometers below the Earth's surface. It is these pressures that contain huge amounts of energy. However, there is also a constant flow of heat that, in theory, can be tapped from literally any part of the Earth's surface. Geothermal fluids are essentially rainwater that has gradually seeped into the ground and is then heated by hot rock. Only a fraction of these heated fluids ever returns to the Earth's surface (in the form of geysers or hot springs); most of it stays deep below ground.

What geoengineers are now seeking to do effectively is to extract these fluids with appropriate drilling technology in order to use it for heating or for the production of electricity. As a source of energy, heat from the Earth appears to have great potential to satisfy the growing energy needs of modern societies. In general, geothermal heat (from the Greek: *geo* = earth, and *therme* = heat) is energy derived from the natural heat below the Earth's crust. Only 20 percent of geothermal heat originates from the time of the original formation of the planet and 80 percent stems from the *ongoing* radioactive decay of minerals, which is why geothermal energy can be considered a renewable energy (Gupta and Roy 2007, Kagel and Gawell 2005). Unlike processes of coal or gas extraction, the energy removed from the source is continuously replaced by natural processes.

Any heat between room temperature and 200 °C can be rendered useful. Geothermal reservoirs are divided into two groups, low and high temperature. Low temperature reservoirs range from about 10 °C up to about 150 °C and are used mainly for heat at the household level. High temperature heat, that is, heat over 150 °C, is used mainly for generating electricity. In general, the Earth's temperature rises by between 17 and 30 °C with each kilometer of depth. Low temperature reservoirs are of particular interest when it comes to connecting geothermal sources to existing or soon-to-be-established infrastructure networks because, as Fox *et al.* (2011) have shown, a large proportion of energy is wasted in processes where the actual need would have been for relatively low temperatures. Fox *et al.* (2011: 3735) show that in the United States, by far "the largest energy use is in the temperature range from 40 to 60 °C, with space and water heating as major contributors." The same holds true for most European countries, where over 50 percent from the final energy consumption is used for heat (UBA 2013). A significant amount of CO_2 could also be saved with the aid of geothermal energy used for heat supply. In general, although electricity is essential for running many household appliances, electricity is the least efficient source for uses such as drying clothes or heating rooms. Thus, geothermal heat – even from relatively low temperature sources – could be an almost perfect addition to more efficiently organized district-based energy utilization.

Geothermal energy has come to occupy a special position among sources of renewable energy because it is available all year round and at every hour of the day and night. As stated earlier, in countries with land located near tectonic plate boundaries (such as Hawaii, Iceland, and northern Italy), geothermal energy has been in use for about a century. Currently, the largest producers of geothermal energy are the United States, the Philippines, Indonesia, Mexico, and Italy. As of 2011, the annual rate of growth globally for this type of energy is about 4 percent (Schulz 2011). Some experts even claim that deep geothermal heat is the most promising option for replacing base load energy, produced up to now by nuclear power (Bloomquist *et al.* 2013, Kagel and Gawell 2005, Paschen *et al.* 2003). These new developments also highlight the issue of political and legal organization – local energy production versus centralized production, dependence on large corporate industries versus energy independence within communities, and dependence on abstract expert knowledge in times of eroding trust in experts versus local knowledge shared in civil society initiatives. However, although geothermal energy appears to offer great potential for future energy supplies, like all new technologies it also harbors major technical uncertainties and risks.

In the case of near-surface geothermal energy, major problems include the risks associated with exploration to find heat sources, unknowns connected with the stability of heat sources, and the lack of experience regarding long-term operations. As a response to the economic risks of finding suitable sources, for instance, the Icelandic government has set up a *National Energy Fund* (NEF) that offers drilling companies a reimbursement of up to 80 percent of the costs of unsuccessful drilling operations. Currently (2014) nearly 100 percent of all houses in Iceland are heated with renewable energy and as much as 82 percent of Iceland's primary energy (62 percent geothermal and 20 percent hydropower) stems from renewable resources (see Björnsson 2010). However, in other countries with less favorable conditions for finding geothermal sources than in Iceland's active volcanic zones, there is no system of insurance in place to cover unsuccessful drilling operations – this is almost certainly one of the prerequisites for coping with unavoidable ignorance or nonknowledge in this context. Additionally, at a political level it is unclear how best to integrate geothermal energy into the existing energy mix. Deep geothermal energy faces even greater risks than other renewable energy sources, particularly in connection with exploration and economic feasibility. The geotechnical risks, including earthquakes, are due in part to a lack of available data for developing useful models and monitoring systems. In most countries, the regulatory framework for sustainable use of the Earth's interior (e.g. the limitations set by mining laws in many countries) is another unresolved issue. Thus, whether one is dealing with near-surface or deep geothermal energy operations, coping with knowledge gaps is the norm. To this end, the following should also be understood as an early foray into research on geothermal energy generation that steps beyond the natural sciences and engineering, and instead highlights some of the cultural issues involved in developing strategies for facing the unknowns and uncertainties associated with them.

APPROACHING GEOTHERMAL HEAT: ART OR SCIENCE?

Some of the perviously mentioned uncertainties in geothermal energy tapping are especially prevalent when it comes to using new drilling technologies to probe deep down into the geothermal reservoirs that exist up to 5 kilometers below the Earth's crust. In this sense, coping with ignorance certainly is the norm when dealing with geothermal energy operations. Rather like today's geological engineers, the fictional characters of Jules Verne's 1863 novel *Journey to the Center of the Earth* have to deal repeatedly with unexpected changes and radical breaks from what they had anticipated and what they had so far accepted as sound science as they set about exploring the Earth's unknown interior (see Gross 2013). Today's geothermal experts and proponents of geothermal, such as Glassley (2010), refer to accessing geothermal heat as a "skill-intensive enterprise" where "detailed knowledge of what will be encountered tens, hundreds, or thousands of meters underground is very rarely available" (2010: 135). In this regard, Frick *et al.* (2010) discuss the many parameters that are largely uncontrollable in enhanced geothermal engineering. A prominent Swiss geothermal drilling expert and proponent of geothermal energy for the future states that at present "there are few deep wells with pre-existing data on which to base the modeling" (Schilliger 2011: 113). A popular science book states even more bluntly that "locating suitable sites [for geothermal energy sources] is more of an art than a science" (DeGunther 2009: 214). This situation is nothing new, of course, in engineering studies. Eugene Ferguson has prominently made the point that no matter how precise the science is, "the successful design of real things in a contingent world will always be based more on art than science" (1992: 193). In other words, moving forward can be done only under conditions of great uncertainty; knowledge is always "perforated."

Unlike any other energy source, geothermal energy is different because at the beginning of a geothermal power project the investment costs are the main source of unknowns. The exploration phase and the test drillings are based on processes of probing gingerly towards success – or indeed failure. After the first stage of exploration (often geological studies conducted by the company involved but more often data available from the literature), the "relevant developer […] will have to decide whether to continue developing the project or not and whether to *assume the risks* of the next phase" (Bloomquist *et al.* 2013: 253; emphasis added). Not only does the project developer have to take the risks, but it also becomes clear at this point that anything and everything can happen (or indeed nothing at all). A white paper published by a Collaborative Research Centre within a major German research institution looking at geothermal energy states the following: "As novel options for resource use in the underground come up, *novel risks* have to be expected that are either not fully understood or are as yet unknown" (emphasis in original).[2] It is generally accepted that decisions need to be taken nevertheless, even in the face of ignorance because, as Bloomquist *et al.* (2013: 266) note: "Computer models that accurately take into account this source of uncertainty to quantify the tradeoffs with competing resources have yet to be developed." These remarks, however, are merely intended to indicate that even experts in favor of geothermal energy production point explicitly to the limits of knowing when dealing with geothermal energy. Taking at face value today's self-descriptions of many geothermal drilling operators and engineers, one gets the impression that the stated goal of advancing research on alternative energy sources, such as geothermal heat, so that these can become a major part of the current energy mix indicates that unconditional belief in science is still very much alive (see Gupta and Roy 2007, Huenges *et al.* 2013, Kolditz *et al.* 2013). Illustrative examples of this can be found in many countries' official statements on geothermal energy. On the one hand, official press releases, telling citizens why they should support geothermal energy, praise it as being highly reliable, economically feasible, supporting national security, and is a widely available and safe energy source. At the same time (sometimes in the same paragraph), they point to enormous research gaps and uncertainties that need to be dealt with in the future.[3] When it comes to overarching issues related to coping with risks and organizing insurance, Miethling (2011) has detected considerable similarities between German, Icelandic, and US geothermal policies despite their different geological prerequisites for geothermal electricity production. Thus, it appears that knowledge gaps and risks do not undermine optimism – indeed quite the contrary. As engineers and hydrologists in favor of geothermal energy repeatedly state, "there are not enough pre-explorations of local specificities available, but we need to move forward nevertheless."[4]

Furthermore, assessments of local geothermal potential (both for deep and shallow sources) are based for the most part on data derived from the literature and not *in situ* from the sites (see Vienken *et al.* 2013).

Despite many more uncertainties and unknowns (including the contamination of groundwater due to drilling, and managing risks and long-term liabilities) and the technical hurdles posed by carbon capture and storage (CCS), there is still a growing optimism regarding the possibility of achieving certainty by conducting research on new remote control technologies and simulation tools for use in the geological substrata (see Mukuhira *et al.* 2013). Giardini (2009: 849) sums up the current situation of geothermal energy utilization in the following succinct terms: "From their outset, EGS [enhanced geothermal system] projects need to be thought of both as pilot projects with scientific unknowns and as commercial ventures with technological and financial risks."

Critical voices, however, point to the fact that a major part of the problem with trying to tap the Earth's internal heat is the poorly understood geology. This appears to be the biggest obstacle for many geothermal experts (see Huang and Liu 2010). A well-known twenty-first-century example of the kind of problems faced by going down into the unknown was a case in Basel, Switzerland, in late 2006. It was already known that earthquakes can occur when steam is removed and water is returned to the Earth, leading to instability along fault or fracture lines. In this case, several tremors were recorded subsequent to the injection of water into rocks at 4–5 kilometers below the Earth's surface near Basel, which prompted concern from local residents. This happened in spite of an allegedly well-established operational method for addressing induced earthquakes and despite a preliminary seismic risk assessment. As this example illustrates, sometimes research engineers have to trust to chance when they do not know exactly what they will encounter. In this sense, intuition and individual experience-driven exploration seem to be a fairly normal part of geothermal research activities. This appears to be particularly true when viewed in the context of general debates about post-normal science (Ravetz 2012) or new modes of knowledge production (Nowotny *et al.* 2001).

DRILLING DEEPER: OLD TECHNOLOGY
AND HIGH TEMPERATURES

The technologies and approaches used for tapping into geothermal energy sources often appear at once quite old-fashioned (e.g. rugged gear that looks a bit like a device for drilling huge fence post holes) and yet very hi-tech and capable of doing amazing things (e.g. drilling 10 kilometers deep). As one representative of a drilling company put it during an interview:

> The technologies we are using are basically 60, in some cases as much as 80 years old. For shallow geothermal sources they are based more or less on those used in traditional well drilling, while deeper drilling requires the kind of technology used to drill for natural gas. The only thing that is a bit new is a slight increase in efficiency due to the coaxial probes.

Thus, the technology used for tapping this source of renewable energy is surprisingly old. This supports David Edgerton's thesis (2007), introduced in Chapter 4, that not only do most inventions take place in the context of practical use but the importance of the old for contemporary social change is much greater than is often expected. Although they still use technology identifiable as a drilling rig, geothermal drilling engineers often adapt and change the direction of drilling in the course of its use and also have to adapt the drilling assembly to new sediment conditions.

Let us consider an example. In many drilling operations for geothermal wells, the drilling assembly (as in gas and oil drilling) is crammed full with electronic devices for controlling the direction of the drilling. The hi-tech electronics and operational tools, however, only work well up to about 150 °C. Furthermore, the drilling technologies that have been adapted from gas and oil drilling need to convey much greater volumes of liquid than in conventional oil drilling so that the diameter of the boreholes is much larger. Thus, the drilling equipment is subject to a high rate of failure at high temperatures (see Finger and Blankenship 2010, Glassley 2010: 135–52, Sohmer 2012). However, economically efficient geothermal power plants in countries such as Germany, Switzerland, and Spain (which are not as favorable as Hawaii or Iceland in terms of geothermal sources) only become a sensible option at temperatures above 150 °C (see Reich 2009: 134–5). In a handbook for geothermal drilling, this problem is expressed thus: "The difficulties inherent in directional drilling are aggravated in geothermal wells because both the electronic tools used to control and survey the well trajectory and elastomer elements in the motors are susceptible to malfunction at high temperatures" (Finger and Blankenship 2010: 46). What is done in cases such as this? Drilling is normally continued nonetheless, albeit with corrections made *ad hoc* in the process (Finger and Blankenship 2010), a strategy also referred to as "seismic prediction while drilling" (Sohmer 2012). A number of unresolved problems remain with regard to directional drilling. These include that of determining the exact position of the measuring instrument in the drilling assembly (close to the bit at the bottom of the string or further away), when exactly to conduct the measurements (given that each measurement is not only a cost factor but also an important issue affecting the general usability of the data) and, finally, how best to safeguard the electricity supply to the measuring devices. To allow electronic tools to work at higher temperatures, the electronics are shielded ("flasked"), a procedure that often renders the accuracy of measurements less certain. Given that it is difficult to secure funding support for research (due to the size of the market and the technical challenges involved) many drilling companies work on their own individual solutions. Technical improvements are thus made *in situ* during operations, and the solutions developed are often not commercially available. This links in nicely with the notion of experimental innovation strategies that are implemented under real-world conditions – such strategies are often developed according to the (spatially and temporally) specific character of the problem at hand and are then corrected as required when circumstances change. This illustrates how the utilization of geothermal heat can be understood as being based on recursive processes of "live" experimentation. This is not to say, of course, that geothermal engineers act without thinking, but that probing the depths of the Earth in spite of unknowns may be the only feasible way of moving forward – or indeed downward.

TECHNOLOGICAL MISHAPS AND
EXPERIMENTAL LEARNING

As mentioned previously, delicate electronic steering tools can easily be damaged by heat or corrosion. Where this has occurred and the electronics have failed, drilling operations often need to be started again from scratch. To be willing to do so requires an attitude towards failure that acknowledges it not as error or as a sign of insufficient rigor but rather as likely and perhaps even unavoidable. Failure – and potential failure – lies at the very heart of an increasingly interdependent world. This understanding of failure in the context of science and engineering refashions the latter as experimental endeavors in which unexpected occurrences are granted a prominent position as the very drivers of modern science and technology *per se* and not merely as side effects or anomalies. Indeed, it is reminiscent of the old professor's stance regarding science that we find in Jules Verne's nineteenth-century novel, where he tells his assistant: "Science, my boy, is composed of errors, but errors that it is right to make, for they lead step by step towards the truth" (Verne 1992: 146). The relation, therefore, between the production of scientific knowledge and its unavoidable side effects must be considered as being mutually constitutive. What we can observe in geothermal drilling operations is the phenomenon of recursively interdependent processes and relations in which skillful scientific reasoning includes the acknowledgement of nonknowledge.

Suggesting a similarly unconditional belief in scientific rigor despite major knowledge gaps, a major European research proposal on geothermal energy utilization from 2012 states the following:

> The major research and testing facilities of [name of a research institution] for geothermal technologies in [name of test site] and for carbon capture and storage in [name of storage site] are being utilized for globally renowned high level research. Both in situ laboratories are unique in terms of both the storage type used in deeper sediments as well as the way they are managed, as they are operated entirely by a scientific institution.[5]

In other words, according to this statement, the results simply have to be accepted because the project is being run solely by a scientific institution (in the sense of not being tainted by extra-scientific influences) – the implication being that everything will be fine because the most difficult problems, including those linked to CCS, will be handled by science. Statements such as this point to a crucial and perhaps widening gap between official rhetoric aimed at the general public and policy makers and the situation of engineers and practitioners on the ground for whom dealing with ignorance is almost the norm. It may also be a reason why practitioners often regard the knowledge produced by laboratory scientists as misleading and therefore tend to ignore it. This may also have consequences for the more general perception of experts in public and, as Mike Michael has pointed out, sometimes ignorance is presented as a deliberate choice by lay people and stakeholders because scientific statements are "perceived as essentially peripheral to, or a distraction from, what the respondent considered to be the real issue at stake" (Michael 2012: 551).

By contrast, in internal debates (that is, not in public statements) geothermal drilling experts often refer to issues that cannot be explained in advance. They say, for example, "You often can't explain why or where you'll find heat. You have a rough idea, but when you actually find it you're surprised nonetheless." As another expert puts it, "Expecting the unexpected, that's everyday normality for us." It appears reasonable to ask, therefore, the depth of geothermal drilling given the lack of data for modeling and the lack of appropriate technologies for coping with such high temperatures. The strategy of moving into the subterranean appears to be characterized, on the one hand, by knowledge based on highly generalized principles (laboratory models, simulations, etc.), which are needed to plan any type of drilling in advance. What it also requires, on the other hand, is knowledge that is highly site-specific, given that unexpected problems may crop up during an operation (as indeed they almost constantly do). Such knowledge often does not exist, however, while generalized knowledge cannot yield the specific information required. As is often the case, however, "engineering can proceed even in the absence of a complete and correct pre-existing scientific understanding of the natural phenomena involved" (Petroski 2010: 49–50). Strategies such as these have also been called real-world experiments (see Gross 2010a, Gross and Hoffmann-Riem 2005), as discussed in Chapter 4. These are experiments that have moved beyond the secure confines of the laboratory and into the real world. They involve complex combinations of social and natural factors where the context of discovery and the context of justification often coincide, so that new knowledge is implemented immediately – as is the case with corrections made to drilling techniques during use. The most important issue in this regard for our discussion is when this kind of real-world experiment fails, the experimenters at least know that something went wrong. In this sense, they were also successful – such failures can make them aware of their own ignorance and this can become a strong motivation to generate new knowledge about geothermal drilling. On a broader level, of course, today's energy transitions may go wrong all the same because technical solutions to reduce fossil fuel consumption are currently not well integrated into the social life worlds of humans and their social institutions (see Jorgenson 2012).

WHERE THE HEAT IS: ON THE LIMITS OF KNOWING THE EARTH'S INTERIOR

Erving Goffman (1967), in his seminal essay "Where the Action is," directed sociologists' attention to the risky and uncertain aspects of everyday life, albeit with a strong focus on situations in which people deliberately seek risk and uncertainty. Since the publication of Goffman's essay, the phenomenon of deliberately venturing into the unknown has become a larger field of research, but reflecting on human exploration of the subterranean world beneath our feet is a unique empirical area still to be explored. Indeed, over the past 20 years many authors have begun to focus on various shadings of knowledge and ignorance (sometimes called "nonknowledge"), as mentioned in Chapter 1. In order to do something successfully, a person needs to have a known residue of ignorance. This suggests a dynamic relationship between knowledge and its flip side, nonknowledge. Nonknowledge is present when there is insufficient knowledge about a certain issue or problem to be solved and when the actors involved are aware of what it is they don't know. Addressing the importance of dealing with unknowns has meant that the challenge posed by nonknowledge in modern societies has moved further towards center stage in many areas of research. Even today, the heat stored below the Earth's crust can readily arouse primordial fears as well as fascination and curiosity about the unknown. Such imaginings have been fostered by medieval illustrations of hell, reports of the unpredictability of earthquakes, as well as by popular fiction stories such as Verne's classic novel about a failed journey to the center of the Earth (Verne 1992). Given this tradition, it appears wise not to wake any sleeping monsters that may be lurking in the depths. Interestingly, however, the fears attached to things lurking below the ground seem to be accompanied equally by a fascination for them, as in the nineteenth century. Drilling several kilometers into the interior of the Earth can be seen even today to hold an innate fascination, not least because it is regarded as a means to explore the "limits" of Planet Earth and of knowledge *per se* (see Evans 2005). This response may well be linked in some way to the recent growing fascination with trolls and elves, longstanding mythological figures in the European imagination. After all, trolls and elves are generally imagined to live invisibly somewhere "underground." This culturally rooted dichotomous attitude towards things that exist below the ground of which we have little knowledge may also have influenced public interpretations and judgments about geothermal energy production, which, compared to other renewable energy sources, still occupies a rather peculiar position in the public imagination. Given the unavoidable uncertainties involved in establishing alternative energy systems, decision making in geothermal energy production and related endeavors necessitates an open acknowledgement that nonknowledge is an inevitable given. Perhaps most importantly, as Andrew Stirling (2010) has pointed out, it is highly irresponsible to acknowledge uncertainty in ways that reduce ignorance to measurable probabilities. In fact, given that knowledge and ignorance are often intertwined with one another, it is crucial, as Stuart Firestein (2012: 173) has put it, for scientists "to learn to talk in public about what they don't know without feeling this is an admission of stupidity." After all, nonknowledge certainly increases when people refuse to admit that they have made mistakes.

To sum up, therefore, in this chapter we have tried to show that an important prerequisite for "successful failure" in tapping geothermal energy is that the scientists and engineers involved need to be prepared to make decisions despite the existence of ignorance. One consequence of this approach would be to undermine the notion that mistakes and failures are necessarily always based on faulty decision making or other human errors. Mistakes would take on a different meaning. This, of course, raises many unresolved questions. If scientists, for example, are now entitled to refer to their nonknowledge as an explanation for errors, when does this serve as subterfuge and when is it a legitimate way of dealing with the unknown?

In order to successfully govern such uncertainties in energy issues – particularly in situations where growing knowledge of environmental processes opens up more and more knowledge about what is not known – decision makers need to find ways of building constructively on the unknown. From a governance perspective, ignorance needs to be taken into account when it comes to decision making. In the next chapter, we will discuss some of the governance strategies and processes that may allow stakeholders to move forward, even in the face of unknowns and novel risks. We examine first a number of significant factors that have played a key role in the perception of a growing need for new forms of governance to cope with unavoidable knowledge gaps and novel risks. This is illustrated by reference to the growing diffusion of renewable energies in several European countries. As part of our discussion, we highlight the relevance of political regulation and its embeddedness in wider forms of governance. Our analysis will also focus on actor networks and their relevance in relation to the process of innovation and the creation of technological trajectories (see Dosi 1982, Garud and Karnøe 2003, Meyer and Schubert 2007, Windeler 2003) within experimental niches, regimes, and landscapes. Additionally, we will place special emphasis on the role of civil society initiatives, processes of participation, and social networks as key driving forces of the energy transition.

NOTES

1 A few isolated studies can be found in English-language publications by economists and modelers (e.g. Miethling 2011, Purkus und Barth 2011, Teske *et al.* 2011). There are also a few on social acceptance

and legal regulations (e.g. Dowd *et al.* 2011, Manologlou *et al.* 2004, Rybach 2010). In addition, there are a small number of anthropologically informed studies – albeit generally dated – conducted in countries well known for their use of geothermal energy, such as Iceland, Greece, and Hawaii (e.g. Canan 1986, Edelstein and Kleese 1995, Kousis 1993), as well as local studies from the field of (mainly physical) geography, starting from the late 1970s (e.g. Pasqualetti *et al.* 1979).

2   These and other quotes are from internal reports and must therefore, for ethical reasons, remain anonymous.

3   For the US Geothermal Energy Association (GEA), see, for example, http://geo-energy.org; for the Swiss Association of Geothemal Energy (Schweizerische Vereinigung für Geothermie, SVG) see www.geothermie.ch; the Federation of German Geothermal Energy (Bundesverband Geothermie, GtV-BV), see www.geothermie.de; and the British Geological Survey, see www.bgs.ac.uk/research/energy/geothermal

4   These and the following quotes are based on field notes and interviews conducted during excursions to drilling sites, geothermal energy workshops, drilling technology fairs, and meetings with decision makers.

5   This is from an internally circulating proposal, which for ethical reasons must remain anonymous.

6

POLITICAL REGULATION AND NEW FORMS OF ENVIRONMENTAL GOVERNANCE

Most research on the development of renewable energies emphasizes the tremendous importance of political regulation as a major driving force in this sector (e.g. Heymann 1995, Jacobsson and Lauber 2006, Markard and Truffer 2006, Praetorius *et al.* 2009, Reiche 2002, Verbong and Geels 2007, Wolfe 2008, Woodman and Baker 2008). This is not very surprising given that researchers generally agree about the considerable influence government policy and regulation has when it comes to the opportunities and constraints affecting environmental innovations (e.g. Huber 2004, Johnstone 2005, Mol 2010). However, it is precisely this issue that has been stigmatized in many social science circles as a result of a number of now infamous debates among media experts, as well as liberal economists who do not shy away from expressing blanket criticism of the energy transition as a series of government failures. Gawel *et al.* (2013) reflect on the reasons for this:

> One reason might be the deep skepticism of liberal economists regarding large-scale government interventions and their related

belief in market virtues. Governments fail and so do markets. To what degree, however, is a matter of debate, which leaves space for ideological reasoning. As a large-scale project relying on state interventions, the energy transition serves as a prime target: an idealized, unfettered energy market may be positioned against an excessively regulated renewable energy market.

(Gawel *et al.* 2013: 128–9)

From a sociological point of view, however, it appears to us to be more important to focus on the connections between the cultural, political, and technological aspects of different energy transition projects in order to highlight the crucial importance of energy in our understanding of social processes. According to evolutionary theories of innovation in this context, political regulation has helped to generate and stabilize sociotechnical niches for renewable energies (Markard and Truffer 2006; Mautz *et al.* 2008). As has been discussed earlier, Geels and Schot (2007: 400) describe such niches as "incubation rooms" for radical novelties. Niches are "protected spaces" intended to shield radical new technologies or experimental projects "from mainstream market selection" and to enable heterogeneous actors to cooperate in a new and innovative way. This type of niche can again be linked to the notion of real-world experiments taking place in the wider society in the sense that new technologies, the development of cities as "living laboratories" (see Karvonen and van Heur 2014, König 2013), and indeed the restoration of landscapes (on formerly contaminated sites, for example) can have multiple functions for humans so that their niche character is not so pronounced after all. Variability and unexpected occurrences that are ruled out as far as possible in laboratory experiments can be perceived as pivotal in the process of understanding real-world experiments (Gross and Hoffmann-Riem 2005); thus, as we indicated in Chapter 3, such experiments should not be understood simply as small-scale niche processes, but as taking place on all levels of the innovation, exnovation, and transition process. Public participation in such projects is frequently seen as a way to improve the quality of implementation (Ansell 2012). Thus understood, these types of experiments "provide locations for learning processes, e.g. about technical specifications, user preferences, public policies, symbolic meanings" (Geels 2004: 912). Another important quality that niches may possess is the capacity to force actors "to deviate from the rules in the existing regime" (Geels 2004: 912). Garud and Karnøe (2003: 281) consider the "process of mindful deviation" as a substantial condition for the emergence – or the deliberate creation – of new technological pathways. In the case of renewable energies, the existence of a politically protected niche was – and is – an important prerequisite for the rise of a new sociotechnical paradigm in the field of electricity generation and supply.

POLICY MAKING AND NON-GOVERNMENT ACTORS

A notable proportion of research on energy sector regulation nevertheless considers government regulation and targeted support for the renewable energy sector to be necessary, but not sufficient, conditions for successful diffusion of renewable energies. We outline the relevant arguments in the following.

First, there is considerable evidence to suggest that the political regulation of the energy sector is embedded in broader institutional changes, including changes in political representation at the national level (after elections, say) and changes regarding the institutions responsible for regulating environmental issues at the international level (Praetorius *et al.* 2009, Reiche and Bechberger 2006). In addition, the interplay between political regulation and other social processes – changing visions about which technologies are considered desirable in a society, emerging public debates on specific environmental issues, and the integration of new social movements into society, for example, calls for careful consideration. Viewed from this perspective, government support for renewable energies is as much the result of a political, economic, and societal institutionalization of environmental protection as it is a driving force in this process.

Second, most studies not only emphasize the role of the government but also seek to include in their analysis different types of nongovernmental organizations involved in the process of adapting, disseminating, or using renewable energies. Such an analytical focus can be useful to illustrate the limits of government policy in the renewable energy sector. Indeed this sector is regarded as a good illustration of the role played by complex forms of governance in which governmental steering is but one component. According to Renate Mayntz (2009: 146) governance can be defined "as comprising all forms in which public and private actors, separately or jointly, aim to produce common goods and services and solve collective problems." Such a reading of governance has been underscored by studies on sociotechnical niche regimes. These studies show that the development and success of niches depends not only on market protection by law and on appropriate financial incentives, but also on the interplay between politicians at different levels of government and individuals from various areas of society, including researchers, technicians, and manufacturers as well as different types of users and – last but not least – representatives of non-governmental organizations such as environmentalists or groups of citizens concerned with promoting renewable energies (Geels and Schot 2007, Mautz *et al.* 2008, Smith *et al.* 2010). Jacobsson and Lauber (2006) focus on specific governance structures in the German context that were developed at an early stage of the "renewables era" and have since been stabilized by ongoing processes of consultation between the different actors involved. In the late 1980s, representatives of non-governmental organizations, citizen groups, members of the German Green Party, and new renewable energy companies formed an advocacy coalition to put pressure on the government. One result was an emergent collaboration with some environmental politicians, who not only supported the expansion of renewable energies but also became an integral part of the advocacy coalition themselves. In an empirical study, Mautz *et al.* (2008) investigated the way in which local governance structures evolved as a result of constructive consultation processes between the different proponents of solar energy (mainly from civil society) on the one hand and local politicians on the other. This study revealed that solar technology was introduced in several municipalities and regions (especially in the south of Germany) in the course of "bottom–up processes." What these processes also served to facilitate – initially at a municipal level – was the joint development of a regulatory framework for break-even feed-in compensation for solar power, as well as the drafting of relevant legislation at federal (national) level (Mautz *et al.* 2008: 78). This kind of collaboration, fostered by the Social Democrat–Green coalition government (1998–2005) in particular, was able to help boost new energy transition strategies. These strategies were aimed at developing better policy measures on the one hand along with better technical options and improved economic conditions for the expanding renewable energy sector on the other. The joint efforts of the advocacy coalition were finally crowned with success when the Renewable Energies Act was passed in 2000 by the German Bundestag and subsequently became a key driver of the dissemination of renewable energies. After the Fukushima incident in March 2011, these joint consultation processes led to yet another "spectacular policy U-turn" (Gawel *et al.* 2013: 123), namely the decision by the government to phase out nuclear power in Germany by 2022. However, this was the same government that, as recently as 2010, had introduced a nuclear phase-in plan as part of an energy policy containing highly ambitious targets for the utilization of renewable energy sources. These included, for example, the aim to have at least 80 percent of electricity generated by renewables by 2050. Viewed in this context, the apparent U-turn of 2011 can be seen to support an overall trend in the German energy system towards a low-carbon, nuclear-free society (see Gawel *et al.* 2013).

The German example shows that the interplay between the emergence of new small-scale, decentralized technologies for renewable power generation (modern windmills, solar panels, small-scale biogas plants, etc.) on the one hand, and a growing societal consensus about the need to tackle environmental problems and take appropriate action on the other, can foster the emergence of new governance structures in the energy sector. The traditional corporatist structure of governance based on close ties between the German state and the interests of the incumbent electricity industry has been challenged for several years now by an emerging network structure of governance in the renewable energy sector that arose out of the early advocacy coalition mentioned earlier (Mautz 2012a). The German case – as indeed the case of energy supply in general – cannot be considered in isolation but should rather be seen as significant in terms of prevailing trends in environmental regulation and ecological modernization in an increasing number of industrialized countries throughout the world. In a study on trends in ecological reform and modernization, Arthur Mol (2010) confirms this analysis when he underlines the changing role of decision makers and what he calls the environmental state:

> The traditional central role of the nation-state in environmental reform is shifting, leading to new governance arrangements and new political spaces. First, there is a trend towards more decentralized, flexible, and consensual styles of national governance, at the expense of top–down hierarchical command-and-control regulation. Second, there is a larger involvement of nonstate actors and 'nonpolitical' arrangements in environmental governance, taking over conventional tasks of the nation-state and conventional politics. [...] Finally, supranational and global environmental institutions and governance arrangements to some extent undermine the conventional role of the sovereign nation-state or national arrangements in environmental policy and politics.
>
> (Mol 2010: 68)

By stating the issue in this way, Arthur Mol and other sociologists who put forward a similar view (see Castells 1996, Urry 2003) are contributing fundamental ideas regarding the state's role in environmental reform while simultaneously prompting the development of a new agenda for sociological research on energy issues in the twenty-first century. Furthermore, studies in online forums and what has been termed the inventive energy user (Hyysalo *et al.* 2013) have given rise to new forms of production and innovation that support the general trend in user-led innovations in the realm of sustainable energy technologies (see Fuchs and Wassermann 2012, Heiskanen and Lovio 2010, Keirstead 2007, Ornetzeder and Rohracher 2006). To reconfigure the term introduced by Hyysalo *et al.* (2013), we would like to refer to citizens active in energy production as "energy prosumers."[1] This term refers to the fact that, especially in the domestic sector, the demarcation between energy supply and demand is increasingly blurred due to the introduction of household or community level technologies. Since these types of technology can be implemented at both an industrial and a household scale, new technical developments relating to both the centralization and decentralization of power supply are becoming more and important. This is what we turn to in the next section.

DECENTRALIZED SYSTEMS OF TECHNOLOGICAL DIFFUSION AND RECURSIVE INNOVATIONS

The interplay between political regulation and groups of actors involved in the renewables sector, however, is related to yet another success factor that remains a key driver of innovation and growth in this field. The key phrase here seems to be decentralized diffusion systems. The rediscovery and early dissemination of renewable energies within the networks of the environmental or the alternative movement of the 1970s and 1980s already displayed the characteristics of decentralized systems of innovation and diffusion, as Everett Rogers (1983) showed. In *centralized* systems of diffusion, innovations generally disseminate in a top–down manner, for example, from the R+D department of large firms down to the everyday user or consumer of a new product – a kind of diffusion similar to a one-way street. By contrast, *decentralized* diffusion systems are influenced and controlled by the users themselves. Innovations emerge in local (i.e. decentralized) contexts, often supported by non-professionals who simultaneously act as the developers and users of an innovation. Thus, local (groups of) actors decide whether or not an innovation is suitable for dissemination within horizontal networks. These social mechanisms are usually propelled by a special mode of communication: "Decentralized diffusion systems are based upon a convergence-type of communication, in which participants create and share information with one another in order to reach a mutual understanding" (Rogers 1983: 346).

During the 1990s, the early systems of diffusion of renewable energies evolved into innovation networks (Ahrweiler and Keane 2013, Kowol and Küppers 2005, Pyka and Küppers 2002) that continued to be characterized by decentralized transfers of knowledge and experience – with decentralized "change agents" as the key figures in the diffusion process. The European renewable energy laws – especially the implementation of feed-in tariffs as the main instrument for promoting renewable power generation[2] – provided a favorable

regulatory framework for the further differentiation and professionalization of these innovation networks. The networks provide opportunities for consultation between the operators and the manufacturers
of renewable energy technologies. While the operators are responsible for the reliability and safety of the *in situ* technologies, the manufacturers are the main driving force behind technical innovations.
Ideally, such consultation processes lead to the constitution of new
technological trajectories (Dosi 1982, Meyer and Schubert 2007,
Windeler 2003) that are progressively stabilized by processes of accu-
mulated learning and the emergence of networks (Ahrweiler and
Keane 2013, Krohn 2007), which, in turn, can be characterized in
general terms as recursively linked experimental processes (Gross 2010a).

In order to illustrate the nature of recursive innovations that help
to consolidate a newly created technological trajectory, we offer first
the example of the development of biogas power plants in Germany.
The emergence of this technology was initially driven forward by the
activities of a large number of non-professional change agents such as
students of agricultural science and members of the environmental
movement (see Mautz *et al.* 2008: 73–5). Today, this is a burgeoning
field of activity involving a host of specialist companies and trained
professionals. These include planning companies and manufacturers
of biogas power plants (most of the manufacturing companies were
set up from the mid-1990s onwards), representatives of professional
associations (e.g. *Fachverband Biogas*) and of regional farmers' associations, and employees in the agricultural ministries of the German
federal states. Up to now, the biogas technology used to generate
power has evolved through a process of learning by doing. Farmers,
the main operators of biogas power plants in Germany, play an
important part in this process: in fact due to a lack of professional
manufacturers in this field initially, some pioneering farmers built
the first small biogas power plants in a do-it-yourself manner. Today,
farmers still contribute substantially towards the further technical
improvement of professionally constructed biogas plants.

The development of modern wind turbines in Denmark during
the 1970s and 1980s can be considered as a second paradigmatic
example of recursive innovations, as described by Garud and Karnøe
(2003) in a comparative innovation study on the emergence of wind

turbine technology in Denmark and the United States. With regard to the Danish case, the authors highlight a "process of creative synthesis" driven forth by "distributed agency," that is, "the presence of multiple actors with different levels of involvement" in an emerging technological trajectory (Garud and Karnøe 2003: 280–1). Garud and Karnøe (2003: 284) describe this process as "bricolage" – a kind of technological development "characterized by emergent co-shaping." They go on to state that:

> designers and producers steadily scaled up designs, all the while incorporating the inputs of the many actors involved. Users offered continual feedback while those in test centers developed evaluation routines that co-evolved with experiences in the field. All the while, policy makers 'modulated' the emergence of the market to keep the technological path alive.
>
> (Garud and Karnøe 2003: 284)

By this means, a "virtuous learning circle" came about that was based on a decentralized system of innovation and diffusion. Perhaps the most crucial element within this process was the close consultation between producers and users. This needs to be understood as part of a classical debate on a technology push versus a demand pull perspective, which, in our case, is "bridged" by the notion of a recursive closure between push and pull. This perspective departs from the linear idea that new technological innovations arise from an inner logic of scientific advances and technological developments and where new technologies are seen as the key drivers in creating novel products. This linear approach assumes that technical progress occurs – sooner or later – "naturally" or independently, and has been put forth prominently by classical authors such as William Ogburn (1922), Jacques Ellul (1964), and Langdon Winner (1977). The opposite view to this is the idea that new technological innovations occur due to market demand pull or, as Gilfillan described it as early as 1935, as an answer to social needs and necessity (Gilfillan 1970). More recently, science and technology scholars have identified representative cases from outside the realm of science. These cases indicate how non-scientists reinvent and transform technological products, the results of which are, in turn, fed back into the development of science and technology (e.g. Beisel and Schneider 2012, de Laet and Mol 2000, Eglash *et al.* 2004). More generally, several strands of environmental sociology, as well as science and technology studies (STS), have developed different models of networks of innovation that suggest a recursive relation between scientific development and technical application.

A characteristic feature of the Danish diffusion of wind turbines was – and in many ways still is – the widespread appearance of "owner–users," usually comprising small cooperatives and individual users. These owner-users soon became a driving force in the diffusion process leading to the installation of a few hundred wind turbines in Denmark by the early 1980s. This in turn prompted a process of recursive innovations, enabled by the presence of many dispersed technical operations and varieties of practical use, which led to a situation that can be compared with what we have referred to earlier as multiple opportunities for real experimentation towards processes of recursive innovation practices. As Garud and Karnøe (2003: 288) put it: "Geographical proximity to wind turbines offered producers an opportunity to rapidly learn about problems and to keep turbines in operation." Thus, "learning by using (…) formed the basis for the gradual design scale-up to (…) larger turbines." In addition, a Wind Turbine Owners' Association was founded, which "began publishing monthly reliability and performance data on most turbine models. These publications created market 'transparency' that forced producers to compete on market-defined evaluation criteria" (Garud and Karnøe 2003). The Danish "bricolage model" of innovation can thus be contrasted with the "breakthrough model," which dominated the early development of wind turbine technology in the United States during the 1970s and 1980s. While Garud and Karnøe describe the emergence of the bricolage model as a success story, they consider the breakthrough model to be inappropriate in relation to the development of properly functioning, high performance wind turbines. In contrast to the process of dispersion and recursive innovation in Denmark, the US case displays the typical characteristics of a centralized top–down model of innovation. As Garud and Karnøe (2003) emphasize in their study:

designers and producers tried to 'leap-frog' the Danes with high-tech designs as developers hyped up future performance of wind turbines to reap greater profits. Researchers at the test center pursued a 'linear' engineering science based technology-push model as their basis for interactions with industry participants.

(Garud and Karnøe 2003: 284)

In the case of wind turbine technology, the "linear" technology-push model actually turned out to be a one-way street: its main characteristic was a lack of consultation between the design engineers in the research laboratories and the practitioners in the producing firms as well as between the wind turbine producers and users. The main reason for the latter was the dominance of a centralized wind farm concept, which emerged in California in the early 1980s and was supported by a statuary incentive structure for investors in wind energy projects (Garud and Karnøe 2003: 288). All this fostered – contrary to the Danish case – the "separation of ownership from usage," which "led to dampened and delayed feedback from those operating turbines to firms that designed and produced them" (Garud and Karnøe 2003).

The polarity between the bricolage and breakthrough models of innovation can be attributed in part to the different industrial legacies of the two countries concerned. As Garud and Karnøe (2003: 295) point out, US industrial development occurred on a large scale and saw regular technological breakthroughs, for example, in the manufacture of mass-produced automobiles, radio, and television, and more recently in the field of microelectronics, computer software, and the new media. Thus, it seemed natural to US energy technology actors that they would choose a similar large-scale manufacturing strategy in the case of wind turbines, too. By contrast, the development of Danish wind turbines was rooted in the "mechanical skill base" of the "traditional Danish collaborative 'small and medium sized enterprise' (SME) industry structure" (e.g. producers of agricultural machinery, boat manufacturers etc.), which facilitated the emergence of the "bricolage" model of innovation (Garud and Karnøe 2003: 285).

The Danish innovation model of wind turbines proved to be superior to the US model – with the result that "despite deploying significant intellectual and financial resources, actors in the US were unable to create a viable technological path (…). By contrast, actors in Denmark pursued a process that deployed modest resources to progressively build up a viable wind turbine path" (Garud and Karnøe 2003: 278). Thus, after a short period (during the early 1980s) in which US wind turbine producers dominated the global market, Danish firms took over and by 1986 had a global market share of about 80 percent. Since that time, the global wind turbine market has altered dramatically; nonetheless, the Danish wind turbine company Vestas is currently still the market leader, its global market share standing at 12.7 percent in 2012. However, this is a far cry from the global dominance enjoyed by Danish wind turbine producers during the 1980s and 1990s. Today, the global wind turbine market reflects a far more differentiated picture, with several Chinese firms among the top ten alongside US firm General Electric (GE), which as a wind turbine producer has acquired a global market share of 7.7 percent (ranked 6 in 2012).[3]

A closer look at the German case shows that producer–user consultation remains an important feature when it comes to innovation processes in the wind turbine industry. Wind farm operators still contribute to the steady accumulation of innovations in this field – not least because they have an existential stake in acquiring systemic knowledge relating to material flaws, instrument failures, and so on. Systems reports on damage, produced in Germany by the Federal Association of Wind Power (*Bundesverband WindEnergie, BWE*), and a system for pooling information in cases of damage or breakdown have become important tools that support recursive innovation in the wind power sector. According to wind farm operators, these tools will lead to increasing transparency when it comes to dealing with the kind of technical problems faced by operators throughout the sector. They also expect to be increasingly able to solve these problems in cooperation with producers and service companies. Last, but not least, they hope in this way to secure a stronger bargaining position when dealing with producers and suppliers (Weinhold 2006).

Compared to biogas and wind power technologies, the solar energy sector is characterized by a peaceful coexistence of professional and non-professional change agents, not least at the local level. Here we

often find craftsmen (e.g. plumbers or electricians), energy consult-
ants, networks of citizen groups committed to solar energy, or representatives of the local municipal government collaborating with one
another to support the dissemination and use of solar energy. Thus,
decentralized diffusion systems emerged from the outset and are still
a major driver of local and regional dissemination of solar panels.
However, the key innovations undertaken in the course of developing solar technology typically occur in the hi-tech laboratories of
solar cell or solar panel manufacturers. These include, for instance,
innovations achieving a more efficient use of materials (e.g. thin layered
solar cells) or an increase in overall energy efficiency of solar panels.
When the solar cell and photovoltaic technology were invented in
the 1950s, the range of applications for which they were deemed useful was initially rather small. Up until the 1970s, photovoltaic cells
were used only in spacecraft and in some niche applications (e.g. toy
cars, watches). Hence, the task facing the pioneers of solar energy
who emerged in the 1970s and 1980s was to open up new possibilities for using this technology. They soon concentrated their efforts on
the problem of how to disseminate solar panels as roof installations
among private users – at first among private homeowners in particular, but later on among other groups of citizens who were willing and
able to jointly purchase solar panels to be installed on larger roofs
(e.g. on top of churches, municipal buildings, commercial buildings,
or apartment blocks). This quest for applicable solutions had (and
still has) an influence on the manufacturers of solar panels and the
suppliers of specific components. Thus, a process of recursive innovations had also been set in motion in the solar energy sector. One
result has been the development of weather-proofed and more robust
solar panels, another is reflected in increasing efforts to improve the
integration of solar panels into buildings (roofs and facades), for
instance by using variably colored solar panels or thinner and more
flexible photovoltaic cells (Mautz *et al.* 2008: 75–6).

The positive impact of renewable energies on regional economies
and labor markets is another factor that helps in their dissemination.
The growing presence of locally- or regionally-based firms involved
in the renewable energy business (manufacturers, operators, service
providers, supply firms, planning companies, etc.), along with the

installation of wind farms or solar power plants on public land and properties means that municipalities can expect increasing tax revenues, local job creation, and an increase in local prosperity. In 2011, the total turnover of the renewable energy sector in EU member states was about 137 billion Euros. The total number of EU-wide jobs provided by the sector in 2011 was about 1.18 million (BMU 2013a: 74–5). Perhaps unsurprisingly, therefore, numerous individuals and organizations outside the renewables sector have started to take an active interest in the diffusion of these technologies. They include representatives of municipalities or regional governments, members of tradesmen's associations or crafts guilds, and trade unions, and have become an integral part of the decentralized diffusion systems that serve to support and improve the effectiveness of government policy measures in the field of renewable energies. Overall, political support for renewables has been highly successful in several European countries. Government regulations in this field – especially renewable energy laws that guarantee adequate feed-in tariffs – helped to nurture innovative potential and supportive capacities that already existed inside the social networks promoting renewable energies. As a result, the diffusion of these technologies has happened more quickly and the range of those involved in the renewable energy sector has become noticeably broader. Globally speaking, there are several non-European countries that also benefit socially and economically from the expansion of renewable energies, most notably China where about 1.7 million jobs were provided by renewable energy technologies in 2011, followed by Brazil (more than 800,000 jobs in the biofuel sector in 2011), the United States, and India (611,000 and 391,000 jobs provided by renewable energies in 2011, respectively; BMU 2013a: 85).

CIVIL SOCIETY NETWORKS AS MAJOR DRIVERS OF THE ENERGY TRANSITION?

The professionalization of innovation networks in the renewable energy sector has been advancing continuously since the early 1990s. Some examples of this include professional associations that have been founded at both national and international level (e.g. The European

Wind Energy Association, EWEA, or EUROSOLAR); an increasing number of new start-ups that have emerged in the various branches of the renewable energy sector (mostly small or medium-sized firms); a growing number of utilities that are now operating their own biomass power plants, wind farms, or solar power plants; thousands of farmers who now operate their own wind turbines, biogas power plants, and/or solar panels; regional councils, trade associations, municipal administrations, and farmers associations that have become involved in order to attract local or regional investors in renewable energies (see earlier); and, finally, several large energy companies that have started to invest in large-scale renewable energy power plants, such as huge (offshore) wind farms and large biomass power plants. Notable differences exist between the different EU member states (and beyond) in terms of the involvement of big energy companies in the renewable energy sector. Germany, for example, is one of the pioneer European states to embark upon the generation of renewable energy, and yet it was only in 2000 that the big power producers – latecomers that had originally firmly opposed political support for the expansion of renewable energy technologies – made their first hesitant investments in the sector. A stark contrast to this is the example of Spain, where renewable energies began to disseminate on a significant scale as early as the mid-1990s, driven from the outset by large Spanish energy companies (Rosenbaum and Mautz 2011: 412).

Thus, with the development of decentralized systems of diffusion, not only was there an accelerated process of learning in terms of the technologies involved but also a broadening of the socioeconomic base of alternative electricity producers. Despite the successful commercialization of the renewable energy sector, civil society initiatives continue to play an important role in several EU countries. This is certainly true of Germany, but also applies to Denmark, Austria, and the United Kingdom. In addition to numerous small and medium-sized commercial enterprises, hundreds (and in some countries even thousands) of non-commercial bottom–up initiatives rooted in civil society are contributing significantly to the growth of the renewable energy sector and to the further dissemination of "green" power generation. What we can observe here is the emergence of a wide range of innovative social practices in the field of energy transition or, to put it another way, the spreading of a cooperative model of power generation and power supply. One key innovation is the so-called citizen-owned energy company – a non-professional (or at most semi-professional) and participatory form of organization set up and funded by a group of citizens and specialized in initiating and operating decentralized renewable power plants. Several studies have been conducted to examine the factors contributing to the success of these civil society initiatives. On the basis of a comparative literature review including Denmark, the Netherlands, Austria, the United Kingdom, and Germany, Schreuer and Weismeier-Sammer (2010) highlight two key factors at the national level:

1   The existence of a strong sociocultural tradition of cooperative organizations in general and/or the emergence (during the 1970s) of alternative energy movements in particular (especially the anti-nuclear movement); and
2   The existence or creation of a favorable legal setting, that not only supports decentralized and small-scale forms of power generation from renewable energies, but also enables voluntary groups and organizations to establish a solid financial basis (e.g. through adequate feed-in tariffs, grants, tax exemptions, the availability of loan capital at preferential rates, and so forth) for operating windmills or photovoltaic panels.

In countries where both of these key factors coincided at an early stage of development of renewable energy (as was the case in Denmark during the 1970s and in Germany from the late 1980s onwards), fertile conditions were created for the growth of civil society activities. In contrast to this, the case of the Netherlands illustrates how unfavorable political conditions can weaken the influence of the alternative energy movement, with the result that "in contrast to small investors cooperatives (founded in late 1980s/early 1990s) have only been of minor importance in terms of installed capacity" (Schreuer and Weismeier-Sammer 2010: 9). A different case is given in the United Kingdom where the early stages of renewables' development were marked by unfavorable conditions for civil society initiatives. Three negative factors coincided in the UK case, namely: (1) "the lack of a tradition of cooperative organizations," (2) "the absence of a strong alternative energy movement," and (3) "an energy policy that has been very much in favor of large scale installations and corporate ownership" (Schreuer and Weismeier-Sammer 2010: 11–12). However, things have changed considerably since then. First of all, there has been a far-reaching change in government policy towards support for renewable energies: drawing on Walker (2008), Schreuer and Weismeier-Sammer (2010: 11) point out, "that since 2000 government support has been available for 'community energy' and that many different kinds of projects have been developed under this label." Second, the change in energy policy has helped to trigger a remarkable upsurge of "grassroots" commitment with respect to local and regional sustainability goals, which increasingly include activities relating to community energy projects. As shown by Seyfang *et al.* (2012: 9), the number of community energy projects in the United Kingdom has grown at an increasing pace since 2003 – there are now not only hundreds of community-led initiatives dedicated to renewable energy generation but also various kinds of "demand-side initiatives" that "are likely to be of a similar order" (Seyfang *et al.* 2012: 2). Seyfang *et al.* (2012: 2) define community energy as "those projects where communities (of place or interest) exhibit a high degree of ownership and control of the energy project, as well as benefiting collectively from the outcomes (either energy-saving or revenue-generation)." However, it is normally very difficult to assess whether these types of community projects can be regarded as a seedbed capable of influencing the wider society on the path towards a more sustainable lifestyle. Prominent observers, such as Seyfang, openly admit that many of the green experimental niches have not yet been able to change mainstream attitudes or practices. In her view, they "are nevertheless important as generators of ecological citizenship values and practices" (Seyfang 2009: 171). In general, it can be said that considerable work is required in order to transfer and adapt the lessons described in the innovation literature to the practical context of renewable energy utilization. Furthermore, as van der Loo and Loorbach (2012) have shown in reference to the Dutch Energy Transition Project (ETP), not only is it difficult to transfer successful niche experiments to the mainstream regime level, it is also problematic that small-scale niche experimentation is enabled by mainstream state structures and therefore remains part of a trend that clearly leads to non-sustainability (see Breslau 2013).

To better assess the specific achievements of community energy, a comparison of the United Kingdom and Germany may offer useful insights. We shall see that there are some obvious differences, but also some remarkable similarities. The most striking difference is the period when a significant community energy movement came into being – in Germany, as shown earlier, this happened in the late 1980s; whereas in the United Kingdom, the rise of community energy began around 2000. As a result, the active participation of civil society in the renewable energy sector is much more institutionalized in Germany than it is in the United Kingdom. Additionally, for some years now there has been a trend in Germany towards a semi-professionalization of community energy projects. This has occurred with the recent formation of hundreds of renewable energy initiatives, constituted legally as "energy cooperative[s]" (Schreuer 2013; Schreuer and Weismeier-Sammer 2010: 13ff.). With the rise of community energy projects in the United Kingdom, however, similarities to the German case become apparent. As in Germany, community energy in the United Kingdom has become a diverse set of activities that go far beyond power generation to also include initiatives in energy efficiency, energy consulting, local or regional energy independence, boosting the local economy, improving social cohesion, and so on. These various activities "are typically instigated and run by a diverse range of civil society groups, including voluntary organizations, cooperatives, informal associations, and partnerships with social enterprises, schools, businesses, faith groups, local government or utility companies," as Seyfang *et al.* (2012: 2) point out with reference to the UK case, although the same applies to the German case as well (Mautz *et al.* 2008). In both countries, therefore, many community energy projects are multi-faceted in terms of their activities and the goals they seek to achieve. In addition to generating "green" energy, reducing carbon emissions, and securing financial benefits, they often strive to enable broad citizen participation in addressing sustainable energy issues, to support the local economy, and to live up to their self-image as pioneers of organizational self-governance and participatory democracy (Heinrichs 2013, Mautz and Rosenbaum 2012, Seyfang *et al.* 2012: 5). This multifaceted portfolio of organizational forms and goals seems to be a general attribute of community energy initiatives, as examples from other countries demonstrate. In Austria, for example, Schreuer (2013) not only finds a variety of legal forms of collective citizen-based ownership in the renewable energy sector, but also identifies a range of organizational goals, such as participation, decentralization, identification, acceptance, and regional value creation, which go far beyond the goal of merely disseminating renewable energy technologies more widely. Another example is Australia, where a number of national-level civil society groups have recently emerged and have initiated a Coalition for Community Energy. Currently (summer 2013), this coalition comprises nearly 40 projects of "many shapes and sizes" (principally in south-east Australia) and recently published a call addressed to the federal government "to establish a $50 million grant program to support the development of community renewable energy projects." The Australian proponents of community energy expect that "support now could kick-start the community energy sector and unlock over $500 million in community investment." In addition, they list a veritable bounty of benefits they expect will be generated: environmental (e.g. "reduced greenhouse gases and pollution"); economic (e.g. "regional development and income diversification"); technological (e.g. "energy self-sufficiency," "renewable energy industry development"); social ("local ownership and decision making," "community building and empowerment"); and political (e.g. "create actors in a renewable energy future").[4] Indeed, these are a set of goals that could apply more generally to community energy initiatives all over the world, as do some key factors of success that can be considered the necessary prerequisites for a desirable development of community energy organizations, such as a supportive policy context (as already mentioned earlier), sufficient resources (money, time, knowledge, people), key committed individuals (possessing the qualities of a "doer"), effective and cohesive group organization, and supportive partnerships and networks (see Seyfang *et al.* 2012, based on a study on British community energy groups).

In summary, it appears that the specific achievements of civil society energy groups are rooted to a large extent in the "hybrid" structure of these organizations. They share this characteristic feature with a wide range of welfare organizations, cooperatives, social enterprises, and similar, which can be regarded as part of the third sector (i.e. voluntary organizations that belong neither to the public sector nor to the private sector of the economy). As a rule, these organizations combine efforts to serve the common good with economic efficiency and forms of self-help addressed exclusively to members. In order to achieve such complex goals, third-sector organizations commonly draw upon a specific combination of resources: social capital (contributed by volunteers), income from economic activities, and financial support from government or public authorities. In a study on social enterprises, Laville and Nyssens (2001) refer to their ability to link seemingly incongruous (or hybrid) perspectives as a specific strength of such organizations: "Social enterprises combine (...) various resources from (...) three poles. Though social enterprises specialise in mobilising donations and volunteers, they can make use of market relations by selling their services and/or use redistributive relations by applying to governments to finance their services" (Laville and Nyssens 2001: 325).

EXPERIMENTATION AT ALL LEVELS OF TRANSITION

Due to their ability to mobilize a specific mix of resources, civil society energy initiatives can be seen as (potential) drivers of energy transition, at least in those countries where favorable framework conditions are in place. If this proves to be the case, it is therefore likely that an expanding array of renewable energy initiatives, cooperatives, and community energy groups will be able to harness sufficient influence to push for a fundamental change towards a socially pluralized and technically decentralized system of "green" power generation and power supply. However, even in countries such as Denmark, Germany, and Austria that have experienced a long period of expansion of bottom–up energy initiatives, it is still unclear to what extent these goals will be achieved in the future. From the point of view of transition theory (see earlier), this will depend (at least) on the following preconditions:

- *At the niche level*: The unfolding of experimental dynamics suited to initiate stable sociotechnological learning curves, as well as to build up and stabilize social alliances with other drivers of a decentralized energy transition, for example, local utilities or private renewable energy companies. This could lead to a self-reinforcing development of niche expansion and niche accumulation that could eventually help to surpass niche status.

- *At the regime level*: The emergence of a competitive niche-regime relationship where expanding sociotechnical niches (or clusters of niches) are able to challenge and, gradually, undermine the incumbent sociotechnical energy regime. However, this type of energy transition requires the niche-based development of a rather mature technological alternative that also works at the system level. It is only under these conditions that the traditional system of centralized (and principally nuclear and/or fossil fuel-based) power generation, still dominant in most industrialized countries, might become obsolete and be widely replaced by a novel system structure based on technological decentralization, economic diversity, societal pluralism, and environmental sustainability. This again can be thought of as part of an experimental process that reaches out beyond the niche level – many innovation processes are characterized by a tight coupling of knowledge production at the niche level and knowledge application at the regime level. The interaction between the niche and regime level, therefore, is in itself an experimental process.

- *At the macro level*: The ability of civil society proponents of renewable energies to affect societal discourses about energy transition, environmental policy, sustainability, etc. as well as to exert influence on politicians or government authorities at the local, regional, and national level. If they succeed in doing so, it could lead to positive feedback loops between niche actors and energy and/or environmental policy makers – perhaps even resulting in improvements to the framework conditions in favor of renewable energies and/or to greater landscape pressures on the incumbent energy regime. In this sense, the energy transition process has turned twenty-first-century energy transition into a large-scale experiment where experimental processes are also interwoven with the landscape level. This can be understood as a fulfillment of Francis Bacon's proposition that science may be able to turn society itself into a large-scale experiment (see Chapter 4) or what we have called the great experiment (see Chapter 1).

In the next chapter, we raise the question of whether there is a flip side to the rapid growth of the renewable energy sector in the sense of specific problems or double-edged outcomes caused by this growth. There is some evidence to suggest that the technical advances and economic expansion of power generation based on renewable energies can be blocked or delayed by specific barriers to diffusion such as those caused by the risks of promoting technological niches or by conflicts emerging from the divergent interests of different actors.

A second issue addressed in Chapter 7 takes as its point of departure the fact that the relationship between renewables and the traditional electricity generation industry has been marked from the outset by competing paradigms often rooted in national and even local cultural assumptions. Renewable energies could only be propagated at first in small niches, which had to be protected by political regulation. Political support and regulatory protection are still necessary, but with the increasing expansion of the niche, the question of system integration at the regime level becomes more acute. This is due to growing incompatibilities between the existing centralized electricity systems on the one hand and the increasing number of decentralized renewable power sources on the other. In Chapter 8, we therefore discuss which different interests and ideas relating to system integration have to be taken into consideration and which solutions are offered by the different actors involved.

NOTES

1 Since Alvin Toffler coined the term prosumption in the 1980s to refer to a close coupling between the production and the consumption of goods, many critical debates around the concept of the prosumer have emerged. For some more recent debates on different areas in society, see, for example, Blättel-Mink and Hellmann (2010), Nakajima (2012), or a critical overview by Ritzer *et al.* (2012). Since

the role of prosumption in the realm of renewable energy has been discussed mainly in the context of user-led innovations, we suggest the notion of energy prosumer to point to the active role of citizens involved in the process of energy utilization.

2 As of 2012, more than 20 EU member states had implemented feed-in tariffs for electricity from renewable energies (BMU 2012: 86). For a critical review of revenue-neutral fixed feed-in tariffs in general, see Lehmann (2013).

3 For an overview, see: www.handelsblatt.com/unternehmen/industrie/windturbinenhersteller-vestas-kassiert-prognose-fuer-2013/7742190.html (accessed August 6, 2013).

4 All quotations are from the homepage of Fund Community Energy, available from www.fundcommunityenergy.org (accessed July 27, 2013).

7

ENERGIES IN CONFLICT

NEW RESTRAINTS AND
OLD OBSTACLES

The EU with its 28 countries has the collective goal of reducing CO_2 emissions by pursuing a continental approach to energy security and sustainable development. Alongside many notable examples of support for renewable energies at a national level, intergovernmental plans also exist to develop major offshore wind farms in the North Sea. There is also a transnational commercial initiative underway whose aim is to set up a "supergrid" in order to supply Europe with electricity from solar power plants and wind farms in the Middle East and North Africa. However, there is some evidence to suggest that the diffusion of renewable energies – driven by social, institutional, and technical innovations – is accompanied by adverse side effects that might conceivably restrict the further growth of this economic sector to a certain degree.

CLASHING INTERESTS AND CONFLICTS WITHIN THE ENVIRONMENTAL MOVEMENT

First, there is an increasing number of conflicts accompanying the accelerated dissemination of renewable energies. This is an indirect result of government support for renewables, particularly in those countries (such as Germany) where feed-in tariffs guaranteed by the Renewable Energies Act are combined with technology-specific rates of digression, that is, year-by-year feed-in tariffs for newly installed wind turbines, solar panels, etc. decrease at a fixed rate. These tariffs can be regarded as incentives for producers and operators to minimize their costs and to maximize the energy efficiency of wind turbines, biogas power plants, and solar panels. In addition to several other possibilities, one way of reducing costs is to set up large-scale power generation, for instance by building huge wind farms or solar power plants consisting of hundreds (or thousands) of solar panels; however, the ongoing spread of large renewable power generation facilities may lead increasingly to problems relating to public acceptance or to other kinds of conflicts. The growing conflicts caused by large outdoor solar power plants and wind farms, as well as by planning applications for geothermal power plants and huge offshore wind farms (in the North Sea and the Baltic Sea) are a clear indicator of this (see Bakewell 2012, Byzio *et al.* 2005, Devine-Wright and Howes 2010, Snyder and Kaiser 2009, Vagiona and Karanikolas 2012).

One predominant type of conflict caused by renewable energies can be described as a local or regional clash of interests. This often occurs in the case of competing interests regarding the utilization of specific areas (onshore and offshore). One example of this is the competing interests of offshore wind farm operators and the coastal tourism industry (Byzio *et al.* 2005: 63–80). In this context, the notion that offshore wind farms are generally less controversial than onshore projects is also challenged by evidence that local people often attach symbolic meanings to coastal areas and feel closely identified by them (Devine-Wright and Howes 2010). In many other contexts, the classical contrast between different perceptions of pros and cons has also played a major role, which includes the role of aesthetics and visual impact, the scope of benefits expected in comparison to the risks, and the role of public involvement in the planning process (see Byzio and Mautz 2006, Haggett 2011, Jepson *et al.* 2012, Pasqualetti 2011). The location of wind turbines in close proximity to residential areas, for instance, is regarded as a source of serious health problems by some people – an accusation normally rejected by wind farm operators.

More generally, many people who live in the neighborhood of wind farms, biogas power plants, or large solar power plants fear a negative impact on their quality of life. In the case of wind turbines, for instance, people are afflicted by noise problems (including subsonic noise) or by visual disturbances (e.g. by the so called "disco-effect" caused by the rotating blades). In the case of biogas power generators, people who live nearby often feel disturbed by the offensive smell. And large-scale outdoor solar power plants provoke some critics to complain about the disfigurement of the rural landscape (see Mautz 2007). In the case of deep geothermal energy, the main adverse side effect appears to be what Paul Slovic (1987) once called "dread risk." Due to an assumed lack of influence on decision making, fears about far-reaching consequences (including induced seismic activities) and a lack of clarity regarding the distribution of adverse effects and potential benefits, many people are wary about renewable energy sources from below the ground. In the case of deep geothermal drilling operations, the highly visible presence of a large drilling infrastructure along with a dependence on abstract expert knowledge can also easily lead to an erosion of trust.

In addition, the expansion of renewable energies has been a cause of conflicts within the ranks of the environmental movement itself (see Byzio *et al.* 2005: 108–65). The results of environmental research, the relevance of efficiency factors, evidence generated by risk assessments and the like are all subject to varying interpretations, and this has led different organizations and individuals to set different priorities. Wind turbines, solar panels, geothermal drilling operations, and biogas power plants are widely seen as technology and not as "nature" – they often intervene in nature by disturbing birds and other animals or by impacting negatively on landscapes and seascapes (see Eichhorn and Drechsler 2010, Krauss 2010, Nadaï and Labussière 2010), causing environmental "costs" that have to be balanced with the ecological benefits renewable energies can provide (Dehnhardt and Petschow 2004, Meyerhoff and Petschow 1999). In the case of wind energy, the conflicts that have arisen around its use have led to a tightening of the legal requirements for wind energy sites. As a result, land for wind farms is increasingly becoming a scarce commodity and is fuelling existing debates about convenient locations and the replacement of existing wind turbine generators with more efficient equipment. Such improvement strategies, however, in turn generate more sustainability problems. Thus the expansion of renewable energies has led to conflicts within the environmental movement that generally follow the fault lines of two guiding principles, both of which play an important role in it. One guiding principle can be described as the ecological modernization of the energy sector, undertaken to protect the environment and the climate. The other guiding principle is conservation for the protection of biodiversity and endangered species.

These conflicts narrow the range of possible locations for renewable energy power plants, thereby exerting pressure on planners and operating companies. However, they are also an integral part of a learning process in society in which the opportunities and limitations of a socially acceptable expansion of renewable energies become apparent. Indeed, given that different individuals and organizations are involved in each particular case, it is highly unlikely that there can be any single, universal solution. Nonetheless, the experiences and learning processes of those concerned about the negative impacts of renewable energies can be expected to help shape broader opinions around the following questions: under what circumstances do people perceive living in the vicinity of these technical artifacts as problematic? Under what circumstances do they perceive it as unacceptable? What kind of solution should be applied in such a case? And which model of participation should be applied in order to ensure a fair process of consultation? To some degree, the viability and transferability of the solutions found (e.g. compromises that are accepted by all sides) will determine whether or not the development of renewable energies will be strongly supported by government policy and society in general in the future (Byzio *et al.* 2005, Byzio and Mautz 2006). With regard to conflicts within the environmental movement, the prospects of finding productive solutions are good, not least because of an increase in mediation efforts within environmental organizations and the lessons learned from conflicts that have been successfully resolved. However, the large environmental organizations are still faced with the difficult task of reconciling their members' diverse preferences and guiding principles, and, depending on one's point of view, this can be considered either as a necessary corrective or as a serious obstacle to the energy transition.

CONSTRAINTS ON DIFFUSION AND UNFORESEEN RISKS OF NICHE EXPERIMENTS

In addition to these factors, there are circumstances in which structural constraints serve to hinder the diffusion of renewable energy technologies. One example is the German biogas sector, which has seen considerable expansion over the last 20 years from 139 biogas plants in 1992 to about 7,500 in 2012, not least because of statutory feed-in tariffs.[1] These plants are, for the most part, operated by farmers who from the outset have been the most important protagonists of the German "biogas boom." However, due to the large sums required to invest in a biogas power plant, the set of skills required to operate one, and the working hours entailed, the expansion of the biogas sector may well soon reach its limits. Given the different sizes and financial situations of farms, along with the diverse qualifications, motivations and mentalities of their owners, only a limited number of farmers will be able or willing to go into the production of biogas (Mautz *et al.* 2008: 103–4). Bensmann (2007: 53–5), who analyzed the development of the German biogas sector, underlines the fact that farmers are the major driving force in the present expansion of this sector, but he also states that, "the number of individual farms that are potential investors" has now become "calculable."

Rather like the small to medium-sized biogas plants operated by farmers, the spread of solar panels for the most part still occurs in line with the decentralized systems of diffusion that emerged in the late 1980s (see Chapter 4). The efficiency of this kind of diffusion is illustrated by the existence of several regions with a higher-than-average number of solar panels on rooftops. The differences with regard to the regional distribution of solar panels are enormous, however. This indicates that the successful diffusion of solar power in regional strongholds, such as the German federal states of Bavaria and Baden-Württemberg, Denmark, France, the United Kingdom, and the southwest of the United States (to name just a few), cannot be readily transferred to other regions. Still, today it is easier to establish the use of solar panels in a rural village than in an urban environment. Alongside the fact that the rate of home ownership is usually higher in small communities compared to big cities, there is also evidence to suggest that people dedicated to promoting solar energy and local opinion leaders generally meet with a more positive response in the context of dense social networks and face-to-face-relationships (characteristic of rural villages) than within the more anonymous and heterogeneous social environment of an urban area. Indeed, data from the so-called German "national solar league" (*Solarbundesliga*) show that the spread of solar panels is a relatively slow-moving process in large cities compared to rural villages – Leipzig, the leading German "solar" city among those with 500,000 and more inhabitants, was equipped with an average 71 watts per capita capacity of solar panels in February 2014. By contrast, the ten leading rural villages (between 1,000 and 4,999 inhabitants) were fitted with average capacities of between 2,416 and 4,360 watts per capita. Moreover, in the category "small villages" (less than 1,000 inhabitants), the four leading municipalities had even reached more than 8,000 watts per capita each.[2] Conrad Kunze (2013) has therefore argued that nowadays it is particularly villages and small towns that are at the center of niche experimentation and energy transition activities, not least because many public utility companies have traditionally been skeptical of (if not actually opposed to) local energy initiatives. Additionally, rural areas can be seen as a crucial locus of energy transition on account of specific types of local coalition (e.g. between local authorities, farmers, and renewable energy cooperatives) that seek to make use of available land for wind and solar farms, as well as biogas plants. Based on studies in rural Italy, Giorgio Osti (2014) has even argued that the diffusion of renewable sources of energy in rural areas can be seen as the most promising way of moving towards widespread use of renewable energy but also as the place where growing tensions over land use loom on the horizon as unresolved obstacles.

With regard to differing levels of intensity regarding sunlight, there is a significant "solar divide" between the different regions in many countries, including Australia, France, Germany, Spain, and the United States. This has inevitable consequences for the average electricity production of solar panels and therefore also for the average feed-in reimbursements that operators of solar power plants can expect to receive. If average incomes are low, as they are in several northern regions of Germany, it is rather difficult – though not impossible – to find prospective buyers of solar panels beyond the limited circles of "eco-idealists" or technology enthusiasts. Since there are higher rates of return in southern parts of Germany, there is greater potential to attract buyers of solar panels who are motivated primarily by financial returns compared to the north of Germany. This target group is indispensable if the development of the photo-voltaic market is to be stabilized into the future (Mautz *et al.* 2008: 102). The German example also shows, however, that such a market-ing strategy can become more difficult when prices for solar panels rise. Solar panel sales among German farmers – one of the most sig-nificant groups of purchasers in this market – saw a marked decline around 2006 due to a jump in prices. Many farmers expected to receive diminishing rates of return and therefore looked for more promising investment opportunities. A few years later, the situation changed radically due to a (continuing) drop in prices for solar panels worldwide, caused mainly by an upsurge of new, heavily export-oriented manufacturers of photovoltaic cells in China. Compared to 2006, when newly installed photovoltaic capacity in Germany was about 840 megawatt peak (MW_p), additional installed capacity between 2010 and 2012 amounted to more than 7,000 MW_p each year (BMU 2013a: 20). Clearly, new groups of investors had been attracted into the market: a wide range of private homeowners, new energy cooper-atives that increasingly came to specialize in operating photovoltaic plants (see Chapter 4), and institutional investors who became more and more interested in solar-based funds or in financing large photo-voltaic projects.

POLITICAL SUPPORT FOR TECHNOLOGICAL NICHES AND ITS UNINTENDED CONSEQUENCES

However, the chances and restraints of dissemination are not only influenced by fluctuating prices for renewables; what also needs to be taken into consideration is that the development of renewable energies has so far been largely a politically driven process (see Chapter 6).

This has been even more the case since the Fukushima incident in March 2011. The German government has decided to phase out nuclear power plants by 2022, while countries such as the United Kingdom and the United States have attempted to construct Fukushima as an exercise in "learning from experience" (Butler *et al.* 2013: 137). This statement points to a belief in nationally specific types of experiential learning as a basis for coping with unavoidable surprise occurrences.

Overall, the success or failure of political regulation in the renewable energy sector depends much on the quality of legislative readjustments and the fine-tuning of government measures and instruments – not least in response to price fluctuations in the renewables market. The previously mentioned example of solar panels shows that renewable energy legislation and feed-in tariffs influence the ups and downs faced by this important market segment within the renewables sector. This can be illustrated with regard to the diffusion of large-scale outdoor solar power plants in Germany – in 2004, the first amendment to the German Renewable Energies Act was enacted, which significantly raised feed-in tariffs for solar power and thus led to a boom in sales of photovoltaic panels in general and in the construction of large-scale solar power plants in particular. To stimulate an increase in energetic efficiency, the amendment prescribes comparatively large rates of digression for the feed-in tariffs paid for outdoor solar power plants. As a result of this change in the mode of digression, a sudden boom in this market segment was followed by a significant slump in sales, further intensified by a rise in the price of solar panels since 2005, as mentioned earlier. Many of the companies involved decided to pursue alternative strategies – some sought to increase their involvement in major projects abroad, for instance in southern European regions with more (intense) sunlight, while others became increasingly involved in building large solar power plants on suitable rooftops (e.g. on top of commercial or public buildings). The obvious reason for pursuing this second strategy lies in the higher feed-in tariffs for roof-based solar panels compared to those for outdoor solar power plants. However, the "rooftop option" does not seem to be a very promising one: many roofs do not meet the structural requirements for large solar power plants. Some projects fail when the owners of municipal or commercial buildings lose interest (Rentzing 2005). As shown earlier, the uncertainties with which German photovoltaic investors were confronted diminished as prices for solar panels fell rapidly. However, from a present-day perspective, this phase of reassuring stability was a transitory phenomenon. In 2012, the German government decided to reduce the feed-in tariffs for solar panels considerably (by about 45 percent), whereas average prices for solar panels went down by only 22.5 percent.[3] As a result, there was a sharp slump in sales in 2013 (nearly 50 percent), accompanied by concerns about the decline of the once-flourishing German solar industry.

Current developments in the offshore wind power sector provide further examples of the kind of difficulties that can arise if innovative technological niches are to be supported by legislative measures. In 2012, about 90 percent of the global capacity of offshore wind energy (5,538 MW) was installed in Europe. Beyond Europe, only China (509.5 MW) and Japan (33.8 MW) have so far built offshore wind power facilities (EWEA 2013: 12). At present, the offshore wind energy market is clearly dominated by the United Kingdom, which in 2012 had 59 percent of total installed capacity in Europe (2,948 MW), followed at a considerable distance by Denmark (921 MW), Belgium (380 MW), Germany (280 MW), and the Netherlands (247 MW) (EWEA 2013: 12). This is not the place to compare in detail each of the national offshore wind power support schemes and their pros and cons; however, a comparison between the United Kingdom and the German case may be instructive. For several years now the moderate expansion of the onshore wind energy sector in the United Kingdom has been accompanied by an ambitious – and evidently successful – government support scheme for offshore wind farms, which, like onshore wind power, is based on an allocation system that uses Renewable Obligation Certificates (ROC) (EWEA 2013: 31). This kind of market support mechanism has helped to attract investors and developers (mostly large power producers from EU member states and Norway) who have been able to set up several large-scale wind farms in the North Sea – a development that will presumably continue over the coming years: "During 2012, construction went on at nine offshore wind farm sites, many of which have held the title of the world's largest offshore wind farm with the prize being briefly held by Walney (367.8 MW), before passing to Greater Gabbard (504 MW) and then to London Array (630 MW)" (EWEA 2013: 31). Overall in 2012, the United Kingdom had "over 14 GW" offshore wind power capacity "operational, in construction, consented or in planning" (EWEA 2013: 31).

In comparison to the United Kingdom, developments in offshore wind power in Germany have been rather modest to date; although Germany is still the frontrunner in Europe in terms of onshore wind energy, it also has ambitious targets for the offshore sector. Since the late 1990s, the German federal government has regarded offshore wind farms as a key technology of ecological modernization within the energy supply sector. In 2010, the federal government adopted a revised national energy strategy that, among other things, proposes the generation of 25,000 MW offshore wind power capacity by 2030 in the German North Sea and the Baltic Sea (BMWi/BMU 2010). However, in 2012, offshore wind farms accounted for less than 1 percent of total German wind power capacity. The situation in the United Kingdom is quite different: here offshore wind farms accounted for about 34 percent of total installed wind power capacity in 2012 (2,996 MW of 8,871 MW overall) (Ancygier *et al.* 2013: 29).

Why is Germany such a latecomer when it comes to offshore wind energy, particularly since it made a hopeful start? In the late 1990s, when the German government decided to promote offshore wind farms, appropriate incentives had to be offered to those wind power companies that seemed prepared to embark on offshore projects. In addition to special feed-in tariffs, the government also gave the companies considerable room for maneuver when it came to choosing appropriate offshore locations for their wind farms. After the Renewable Energies Act had been passed in 2000, numerous licensing procedures for offshore wind farms were set in place (more than 30 during the following two years alone; Byzio *et al.* 2005: 31). A considerable number of applications have been approved by the relevant authorities to date. If all these projects were to be realized, nearly 9,000 MW offshore wind power capacity could be installed in the coming years (BMU 2013b: 12). However, as shown previously, only a small proportion of this capacity has been implemented so far.

One reason for this is that the government's promotion of offshore wind farms led to some unintended outcomes. First, several of the offshore projects initially planned triggered disputes and met with opposition from conservationists who feared an increase of environmental stress for seabirds and sea mammals, as well as a serious threat to the ecologically unique – and environmentally protected – mud flats of the North Sea coast (Mud Flats National Park). Second, a large number of people living on the North Sea islands and in the coastal areas remained skeptical about the expected economic results an offshore boom might bring, especially with regard to regional tourism and the fishing industry. Representatives of the tourist industry argued that offshore wind farms would deter many visitors to the area, and would therefore cause serious problems for a region whose economy depends to a great extent on an expanding tourism sector. Similarly, the region's fishermen believed it likely that if important fishing areas were to be occupied by large offshore wind farms, this would damage their livelihoods. In addition, many coastal inhabitants were afraid that some of these wind farms might be located near to heavily frequented shipping lanes in the North and Baltic Seas, thus increasing the risk of shipping accidents and ecological disasters in the vicinity of the coast.

As a result of these strong reservations, local debates were soon marked by conflicts between the promoters of offshore wind power on the one hand and the opponents of these projects (e.g. environmentalists, representatives of seaside resorts, fishermen) on the other (Byzio *et al.* 2005: 91–107). Clearly, there was a need for further legislative revisions. Due to the previously mentioned conflicts, there was no realistic chance of building wind farms in less cost-intensive near-shore locations (at a maximum distance of 15 or 20 kilometers from the coastline) as practiced in the United Kingdom, Denmark, and Sweden. Thus, nearly all the German offshore wind farms that are either already installed, under construction, or planned are located far out in the open sea (in some cases 60 or more kilometers from the coastline).[4] Alongside the fact that an appropriate and economically feasible location for the projects was (and is) not easy to find, the wind power companies soon had to deal additionally with rising prices for steel (which is needed in large quantities to build wind turbines) and for some other primary products. Only one year after the first amendment of the Renewable Energies Act was introduced (in 2004), representatives of the wind power industry called for further revisions. They argued that prospective projects "could barely be financed" on the basis of the present – already enhanced – feed-in tariffs (9.1 cents/kWh) for offshore wind farms (Lönker 2005: 12). A further revision to the legislation followed in the fall of 2006: the German grid operators were bound by law to assume the costs of connecting offshore wind farms to the power grid. As a result, many in the wind power industry fully expected that it would now be feasible to achieve profitability for German and Dutch offshore projects (see Vasi 2010). Despite this, it was only in April 2010 that the first German offshore wind farm was completed – a pilot project with a capacity of 60 MW, realized by a joint venture of several large German power companies (BMU 2013b: 12). In 2011, German power company Energie Baden-Württemberg AG (EnBW) started operating a wind farm in the Baltic Sea (with a capacity of just 48.3 MW) and in September 2013, the third German offshore wind farm, known as BARD Offshore 1, was finally completed: a 400 MW power plant, about 100 kilometers northwest of the North Sea island of Borkum, and reaching a depth of about 40 meters (BMU 2013b: 12). Given the still-sluggish progress of the offshore wind energy sector in Germany based on the ongoing reluctance of power companies and institutional investors to invest in this sector, the federal government decided once again to enhance the feed-in tariffs for offshore wind power. Thus, a recent amendment to the Renewable Energy Law (adopted in January 2012) grants a feed-in tariff of 19 cents/kWh for the first 12 years, as long as operations begin before January 2018. After this deadline, the feed-in tariff will fall to 15 cents/kWh (BMU 2013b: 13–14) in the first 12 years.[5] As a result, offshore wind power is currently the most expensive form of electricity generated by renewable energies in Germany – even more expensive than electricity from photovoltaic panels, where feed-in tariffs range from 9.47 to 13.68 cents/kWh (as of January 2014).

However, despite being the best-paying renewable energy source, there has been no German offshore boom to date. Many prospective investors still seem to be skeptical about the financial benefits that are said to accrue from investments in offshore wind farms. New problems have arisen due to the technical challenges involved, as well as the huge costs of connecting offshore wind turbines in the open sea to the power grid and laying the necessary power transmission cables to the coast and beyond. These problems have caused a serious delay in the construction of transmission cables and have thus created a further hurdle on the way to achieving a significant offshore wind power supply. The leading protagonists in the offshore wind power industry, therefore, have already demanded further enhancements to statutory support schemes in order to have greater certainty when planning future offshore projects (Wehrmann 2013).

To sum up, there are several important differences in the framework conditions governing offshore wind power in the United Kingdom and Germany. While Germany has sought to be a pioneer in both onshore and offshore wind power, it underestimated the technological and financial dimensions involved, as well as the necessary statutory support for such an undertaking. In addition, the German government, as well as the businesses involved in the initial phase of offshore wind farm planning, underestimated the severity of the conflicts (environmental and economic) provoked by their agenda. By contrast, the United Kingdom entered the offshore wind power business a few years later than Germany, and was therefore able to benefit from the technical insights and initial experiences gained from existing operations, especially the pioneering Danish offshore wind farms. Moreover, the United Kingdom was confronted much less than Germany with conflicts stemming from local resistance to offshore wind farms and also because British offshore planners and permit authorities did not have to consider ecologically highly sensitive coastal regions like the German Mud Flats National Park. In these circumstances, it has been possible to embark on technologically and financially less-risky near-shore projects in the United Kingdom, which has facilitated the country's first steps into the implementation of maritime wind energy technologies. Finally, UK government support schemes for offshore wind farms have been more effective from the outset than those in Germany in terms of motivating investors to put money into offshore wind farm projects and prompting wind turbine manufacturers to develop feasible technologies for offshore usage.

The previously mentioned cases of photovoltaic panels and offshore wind farms underline the fact that statutory support for innovative niches opens up new opportunities for more sustainable technologies and, ultimately, for regime change in the electricity sector. However, it also entails some risks – especially the risk of failing to ensure that new technologies will continuously disseminate and reach a favorable market position. To minimize this risk, it is necessary to undertake appropriate revisions to policy measures and instruments, as exemplified by the gradual enhancements of financial and legal conditions for offshore wind farm operators. Nevertheless, the policy makers are caught in a dilemma: the strategy of providing continuous enhancements to favor a specific technology – one that up to now has been highly successful in the case of renewables – can quickly mutate into an inadequate policy scheme if the endogenous potential of a new technology turns out to be overestimated (see Huber 2004). It is therefore impossible to rule out the possibility that political support for certain renewable energy technologies – contrary to the intentions of renewable energy support schemes – might end up being caught in an enduring "subsidies trap."

NOTES

1 For these data, see: www.unendlich-viel-energie.de (accessed May 13, 2014).

2 *Solarbundesliga* is published by *Solarthemen*, a news agency specializing in renewable energy, in cooperation with *Deutsche Umwelthilfe e.V.*, a non-commercial NGO ("German Environmental Aid"). For these data, see www.solarbundesliga.de (accessed February 28, 2014).

3 www.solarwirtschaft.de/fileadmin/media/pdf/bnetza_aktuell_kurz.pdf (accessed November 1, 2013).

4 A figure shown in a report published by the European Wind Energy Association (EWEA 2013: 10) illustrates that the average distance to shore of German offshore wind farms under construction is considerably larger compared to offshore wind farms under construction in the United Kingdom, Denmark, or Belgium (in 2012).

5 After this date, the feed-in tariff for offshore wind power will be 3.5 cents/kWh (BMU 2013b: 13).

8

INTEGRATING RENEWABLE ENERGIES INTO EXISTING ELECTRICITY SYSTEMS

As long as renewable energies made only a marginal contribution to power generation as a whole, the question of how to integrate small, decentralized operations into the existing electricity system was considered of secondary importance. For the same reason, the variable output produced by wind turbines and solar panels (intermittent power sources vulnerable to unpredictable wind conditions and seasonally variable amounts of sunlight, respectively) was initially not a major concern.

With the recent accelerated expansion of renewable energy sources, however, this question has become much more urgent. Incompatibilities between this new mode of power generation and the established system of power supply are likely to increase and become a serious obstacle to the further dissemination of renewables. Thus, finding the most efficient ways of integrating renewable power sources into the electricity system has become a crucial challenge in order to avoid "bottlenecks" and slowdowns in the course of energy transition.

On the one hand, the issue of system integration has a far-reaching "visionary" aspect, insofar as many supporters of renewables (e.g. proponents of citizen-owned power plants or community energy) are keen to develop a completely decentralized system of power generation and distribution. An alternative, equally ambitious vision is that of a transcontinental power grid based mainly on linking together large-scale renewable power plants (see later).

On the other hand, the complexity of the present energy system suggests that it could be useful to link laboratory research, planning, and simulation models to real-world experimentation in order to provide novel insights that probably cannot be achieved any other way. Whereas modeling and laboratory research practices are not normally dangerous to the outside world, real-world experiments that take place in and with society necessarily shift some of the risks involved onto society itself. Failures attributed to these risks thus become a major issue in societal debates over the acceptance of new scientific research and technologies. Although they can serve as a significant learning opportunity, they also pose a major challenge in terms of their consequences and the allocation of responsibility for these. However, today's politically driven imperative to forge ahead with renewable energy research in the context of its application (society) seems to resonate well with Henry Petroski's description of mishaps in engineering. As Petroski (2012: 45) puts it: "Every failure is a revelation of ignorance, an accidental experiment, a found set of data that contains clues that point back to causes and further back to mistakes that might have been made in design, manufacture, and use." Major energy transitions, of course, may go wrong all the same; however, if the types of niche experimentation described earlier in this book are not allowed to take place, there is no way of testing the feasibility of significant options of energy generation and use, a process that may even give rise to previously unimagined alternatives that are ecologically, economically, and socially innovative. In other words, if processes such as a politically supported transition to renewable energies are combined with this understanding of experiments, then unexpected events need not necessarily be rendered as purely negative but actually as crucial in order to learn from them and thus help create better and safer technological solutions. When understood in this way, system integration also needs to be conducted in a pragmatic and experimental manner, not least because the expansion of renewable energies and the associated need to integrate decentralized power sources into the system of electricity supply puts pressure on a range of actors – not only on the advocates of renewable energy but also on the protagonists of the conventional energy system. Optimizing this process of system integration is surely one of the most urgent tasks to be addressed in order to ensure that renewables constitute an ever-increasing share of overall power generated. It is a task that displays all the characteristics of a real-world experiment, as the following pages will show.

THE CHALLENGES OF SYSTEM INTEGRATION: EXPERIMENTAL STEPS

Perhaps the most crucial challenge is to introduce greater flexibility to the existing system of power generation and power supply. With regard to conventional power generation, greater flexibility means that existing coal and nuclear power plants, which generally operate according to base load energy requirements, need to be replaced step-by-step by more flexible power plants, for example, by gas turbines. If this is not done, there will soon be a looming system conflict – because their inflexible mode of production makes them unable to respond appropriately to a steadily increasing share of intermittent power generation derived from wind energy or solar power plants, base load power plants would "choke up" the power lines, thereby restricting the feed-in capacity of electricity from renewables (SRU 2009).

With regard to renewable power generation, the task of greater flexibility comprises a number of different measures and innovations. First, the operators of renewable power plants will need to adopt a range of necessary technical measures relating to system stabilization in order to guarantee a stable and secure but also safe power supply. This applies especially in the case of "priority dispatch." Priority dispatch, as regulated by the German Renewable Energies Act, for example, means that wind farm operators, owners of biogas or solar power plants, etc. are entitled to generate and feed in electricity preferentially into the grid, irrespective of the present demand for power or of changing grid situations. However, due to the needs of secure power supply (e.g. to avoid overloading the grid or having sudden voltage fluctuations),

German operators of renewable energy plants (of wind farms in particular) have for some years been obliged to install technical equipment capable of preventing grid instability by providing and balancing energy. The latter requires flexibility in the sense of temporarily foregoing priority dispatch: upwards control of power balancing can only "be provided by partly curtailed wind farm generation, kept within a pre-defined capacity band and made available within seconds" (EWEA 2005: 101).

A present-day example to illustrate the experimental – and often conflict-laden – aspects of these growing demands for flexibility is the wind farm feed-in control practiced by grid operators in some North German regions to prevent temporary overloading of power lines, and to better adjust regional wind power generation to actual demand. The wind farm feed-in control has often become a source of conflict. On the one hand, grid operators are interested in the most effective use of the power grid, technically and economically; on the other hand, wind farm operators are interested in keeping their losses of feed-in payments as low as possible. The German wind energy industry has repeatedly complained about losses of income in the order of millions of Euros due to grid operators occasionally scaling down the output of wind farms or temporarily disconnecting a large number of wind turbines from the power grid (Mautz *et al.* 2008: 122). Several of these conflicts – including controversies over the legality of scaling down wind farm output and disputes about financial compensation for reduced feed-in payments – have been brought to court. For some years now, the wind energy industry has been putting legal pressure on the grid operators to force them to optimize or extend their power grids, the aim being to ensure that increasing amounts of wind power can be transmitted in the future.

The experimental aspect of these controversies finds expression in the fact that wind farm feed-in control has led some protagonists in the wind energy industry to push for an alternative solution. One pioneering project that embodies this solution has already been realized in the north-eastern corner of the German federal state of Brandenburg: several wind farms are linked together by means of appropriate IT-based process control and by power lines that are the property of the wind farm operators themselves. The declared objectives pursued by the advocates of so-called networked power plants are independence from the established grid operators and provision of a steadier and more reliable feed-in of wind power into the transmission grid. Such networked plants, they argue, can serve to enhance the capacity of the regional power grid while simultaneously increasing the potential volume of regionally-generated wind power (Mautz *et al.* 2008: 123).

A further experimental step in this direction is the combined renewable power plant, which is also based on the principle of adopting technological developments in the IT sector. A number of people in the renewable energy sector, partly in cooperation with scientific institutes, municipal utilities or network operators, are pushing forward this innovation because they see it as a way of avoiding delay in the ongoing expansion of renewable electricity. The basic idea behind it is the connectivity and centralized control of *different* decentralized power sources, for example, wind energy, geothermal heat, photovoltaic panels, and biogas plants (combined with an energy storage device, such as a pumped storage hydro power station, if possible). The aim of this connectivity is to stabilize power input and to adapt it to the consumption curve. Apart from creating an integrated grid, the intention is also to advance the market integration of renewable electricity. As the electricity from combined renewable power plants can be delivered reliably and predictably, it is also suitable for sale on the European Energy Exchange (EEX).[1] The incentive for the operators of these so-called virtual power plants is that they can expect to obtain higher revenues for their electricity on the energy exchange than they would get from the legally fixed feed-in tariffs. In sum, therefore, the connectivity and market integration of renewable energies, made possible by information technology, creates beneficial conditions for the integration of ever greater capacities of renewable power within the grid and thus for greater energy consumption. It is therefore an important – albeit still experimental – step towards ensuring the dominance of renewable energies in future power supply.

Additionally, there is another technological innovation that may contribute in an even broader sense to the task of system integration, namely, the "power to gas" technology. This technology has a wider range of potential applications compared to the combined renewable power plant, insofar as power to gas would be able not only to stabilize the feed-in of wind and solar power into the grid, but would also help to expand considerably the share of renewables used in heating and fuels. Power to gas refers to a specific, and more flexible, kind of energy storage technology where temporary "spare" quantities of renewable electricity are used to produce hydrogen (H_2) by electrolysis. If required, the hydrogen can be converted to synthetic methane gas (CH_4). This methane gas, and a certain amount of hydrogen, can be stored within the existing natural gas supply infrastructure (gas grid, gas stores) and is available for further use, chiefly in three ways. First, the gas can be reconverted to electricity at times of high demand. Second, the gas can remain within the gas grid to be used for home heating, cooking, etc. Third, the gas can be converted to fuel and be used in cars ("gas to liquid"). Power to gas seems to be a promising technology insofar as it broadens the possible applications of renewable electricity. However, it is still at the experimentation stage – with all the uncertainties this involves. In recent years, a few pilot projects have been started up in a number of European countries, including Denmark, Germany, France, Spain, the Netherlands, Italy, and Norway; outside Europe there is a "power to gas and gas to power" plant in Argentina that has been in operation since 2008.[2] Presently, the greatest uncertainties affect the extent to which it is possible to apply experience from fairly small pilot projects to the development of large-scale power to gas technologies. These uncertainties include issues such as the potential risks of cost increases and the level of energy efficiency, as well as the degree of technical reliability that can be achieved by this technology. These are serious issues, especially because the previously mentioned electric–chemical conversion techniques usually involve considerable energy losses. This means, for example, that when electricity is converted into hydrogen and hydrogen back into electricity, the efficiency factor declines in the process.[3]

In the case of geothermal energy, the utilization of existing infrastructures can be seen as a crucial strategy to ease the transformation towards renewable energy. Existing gas heating systems, for instance, could be merged so that the relevant infrastructures could be retrofitted to receive energy supplied by enhanced or engineered geothermal systems. Thus, carrying the extra costs of drilling (after all, drilling costs still harbor the highest uncertainty in geothermal energy utilization) and the completion of the wells would be the only additional tasks required to connect a heat exchanger to the existing infrastructure.

A NEW "DOMINANT DESIGN"? THE ROLE OF POLITICAL REGULATION AND CONSUMER BEHAVIOR

There are currently several competing technological options being explored with the aim of achieving better system integration of decentralized renewable energies.[4] In the context of evolutionary models of innovation, this is a typical indicator of the fact that these technical developments are still at an early – experimental – stage in the overall innovation cycle. Following Tushman and Rosenkopf (1992) as well as Weyer (2008: 167–71), the selection of a "dominant design" out of a multitude of new technological options is not guided merely by technical logic – at least not in the case of complex systemic solutions – but is influenced to a greater or lesser extent by social and political processes. Thus, the choice between rival designs is made in the course of a sociopolitically framed negotiation process during which networks or coalitions of different interest groups (scientific and/or technological communities, alliances of firms, user/consumer groups, politicians, etc.) play a crucial role. This process tends to end in a compromise out of which a new "dominant design arises."

At present, the competing innovations in the field of renewables system integration are still in the "fermentation" phase (Tushman and Rosenkopf 1992) – this means that there are considerable uncertainties around whether any one of these solutions will predominate in the future. In addition to the capacity for innovation and the economic strength of the companies involved, there are at least two further important factors that will probably influence the emergence of a new "dominant design": political regulation and consumer behavior.

The regulatory requirements that are needed if renewable energies are to be adequately integrated into the system of power supply go beyond previous support mechanisms for renewables (e.g. specific feed-in tariffs for each individual technology). Instead, system integration requires innovative measures at the level of network regulation. According to Bauknecht and Voß, who refer to the United Kingdom as the "homeland of the standard model of network regulation" (2009: 192), such innovations are necessary in the new situation. The "standard model" to which they refer was originally developed for the electricity sector in the United Kingdom in the late 1980s, with the aim of promoting liberalized electricity markets and has since been widely adopted at an international level and is described by Bauknecht and Voß as follows:

> It is based on privately owned, profit oriented network operators that are unbundled from other parts of the industry and economic regulation through independent, sector-specific regulatory authorities that seek to mimic the pressure of competitive markets, and give network operators incentives to become more efficient. The standard model of network regulation focuses on one particular aspect of the energy system, namely the economic regulation of networks, and is separated from other aspects.
>
> (Bauknecht and Voß 2009: 219)

The question is whether such an efficiency-oriented regulatory framework based on financial incentives is fully compatible with the policy goals of further expanding and integrating renewable energies into the overall energy system. In response to Bauknecht and Voß (2009), there is cause to be skeptical, especially if efficiency is defined in narrow terms as short-term efficiency, that is to say, in terms of the reduction of operating costs and tariffs. Incompatibilities can be expected with regard to the following points at least.

Decentralized renewable power plants have to be connected to a network level – the distribution grid – that, according to Bauknecht and Voß, was "not designed for that purpose" (2009: 210). Thus, the further dissemination of renewable power plants requires a long-term and fundamental restructuring of the grid and of grid operations – a problematic goal from the perspective of short-term efficiency. Without special incentives for connecting distributed generation, grid operators may well be reluctant to support the further diffusion of small decentralized power plants or to improve the grid infrastructure for that purpose. Conflicts and tensions between network operators and advocates of renewable energy, as mentioned earlier, could be the consequence. This is especially likely when it comes to the task of integrating distributed generation into the overall system. Whether pioneering projects, such as those mentioned earlier, set a precedent and help to further stabilize the ongoing development of renewable energy will depend on whether or not an adequate regulatory framework is created for this kind of innovation, for instance, via financial incentives for wind farm operators who contribute to grid stabilization, or for electricity generated by combined renewable power stations or power to gas technologies. As Bauknecht and Voß (2009: 219) point out, "a transformation to a sustainable electricity system requires an integrated approach, coordinating changes in different parts of the system, and taking into account long-term structural effects of today's regulatory actions." In addition to discussing the shortcomings of the "standard model of network regulation," Bauknecht and Voß describe a changing situation in Britain since the late 1990s that has involved "reopening the 'standard model'" (2009: 205). The key drivers in this include a drop in investment in the grid due to liberalization as well as a gradual increase in distributed power generation (DG) in the United Kingdom, which have forced the need to adapt (or even transform) the grid onto the agenda. "Attempts to integrate new developments like DG into the standard model have thus started to put the standard model under pressure" (Bauknecht and Voß 2009: 211), and have triggered "an increasing number of innovative network concepts" (Bauknecht and Voß 2009: 212). The latter stems in part from the Electricity Network Strategy Group (ENSG), which was set up in 2005 and has the job of supporting the transition of power grids "to a low-carbon future" (Bauknecht and Voß 2009: 213).

As already emphasized, it is important to consider system flexibility as an overarching goal of the various innovative technologies and (regulatory) measures designed to achieve system integration of renewables. However, the task of flexibility is not limited to possessing "smart" system technology, such as IT-based process control of (combined) decentralized power generation and transportation, supported by a proper regulatory framework. What also needs to be taken into account is that the development of a flexible and efficient decentralized power system also relies on energy consumers who are willing and able to adapt their consumption behavior to the requirements of such a newly designed power supply system. The behavioral aspect is an important one because flexibility and efficiency mean bringing the power input of distributed generation – as far as possible – into line with the consumption curve in order to avoid redundant power production or interruptions in power supply.

Ensuring that energy consumption becomes more flexible and efficient is no easy task, however. Nowadays, most consumers still perceive electricity to be a "low interest product" (Praetorius *et al.* 2009: 138), insofar as "they ignore its dimensions, main drivers, cost and environmental consequences" (Praetorius *et al.* 2009: 144). By contrast, transitioning towards a decentralized and well-integrated system of renewable energy supply would require consumers who perceive electricity as a "high interest product" and use it accordingly. This would mean, for example, that consumers become active participants in demand-side management, an important component of balancing supply and demand appropriately within the electricity system. Demand-side management is a technique aimed at optimizing the integration of fluctuating distributed generation from wind turbines or photovoltaic panels into the grid system. Financial incentives (price signals) can serve to motivate consumers to adapt their demand to the intermittent input from renewables. Intelligent process control of the power grid (smart grid), as well as smart meters at the household level, are indispensable prerequisites for sending short-term price signals and information about a household's energy consumption. If the system works well, all sides can expect to benefit: households save energy and money; the grid operator can reduce his demand for expensive "balancing energy;" and energy producers can operate their power plants in a more efficient way and avoid expensive load peaks. Thus, becoming an "active energy consumer" means taking an active interest in energy efficiency and energy saving at home, using smart metering and smart electric household appliances appropriately, or becoming an "energy prosumer" (see Chapter 6) who operates their own photovoltaic panels or micro-combine heat and power (CHP) unit. This all requires a new kind of commitment to the objectives of energy transition as well as the willingness and the ability to change one's behavior. Studies have shown that there are considerable barriers impeding behavioral change towards a more sustainable lifestyle, not least in the field of energy consumption (Mautz 2012b). As Praetorius *et al.* (2009: 138) emphasize, "normal daily energy consumption is completely unconscious." In other words, behavioral change in this context is by no means self-evident; rather, it requires – alongside appropriate political frameworks and support measures (e.g. feedback devices displaying energy consumption; Praetorius *et al.* 2009) – a conscious process of questioning and changing certain cultural patterns, normative perceptions, and every-day routines and cognitive framings (Mautz 2012b). There is some evidence to suggest that the expanding group of "energy prosumers" could play a pioneering role in this kind of behavioral change, espe-cially where the producers themselves consume the electricity they have produced (using photovoltaic panels or micro-generation) in their own household, but also in cases where local citizens participate in a renewable energy cooperative or a citizen-owned power plant, etc. These individuals, households, or citizens' groups presumably perceive electricity as a high interest product, and the evidence sug-gests that their involvement in decentralized power generation serves to heighten their awareness of energy efficiency and energy saving in everyday life. What is not yet clear is the extent to which the activities of these citizen pioneers will result in a broader process of learning in society that takes place parallel to changes in energy consumption more generally. One way of advancing the process of dissemination and energy transition could be to provide appropriate political sup-port for strategies of decentralization so that an increasing number of citizens and households are motivated to participate in distributed power generation and consumption.

To sum up, the integration of renewable energies into the broader system of energy provision consists of a complex set of real-world experiments involving a wide range of social actors – power producers and providers, grid operators, consumers, regulators, developers of innovative technological solutions, and several more. The challenges are huge, and the chances of success are uncertain. As we have seen, a far-reaching decentralized solution requires the cooperation of a host of local and regional actors as well as a considerable number of supportive consumers. Alongside this approach, however, another potential solution is under discussion. It is no less ambitious but follows a different systemic logic: the "supergrid" solution.

THE "SUPERGRID" SOLUTION: AN ALTERNATIVE PATH TOWARDS SYSTEM INTEGRATION?

The basic idea of a "supergrid solution" is to produce electricity from renewable energies on a large scale, while exploiting comparative advantages at those locations where the efficiency of power generation is greatest, for example, by operating offshore wind farms in the North Sea, concentrating solar thermal power plants in North Africa, hydropower plants in Norway, geothermal power plants near tectonic plate boundaries, and biomass power plants in Eastern European countries. The idea behind this "supergrid," which consists of high-voltage direct-current transmissions, is that only some of the electricity generated in large-scale plants would be used in the respective country of origin, the rest would be transmitted – with minimal losses along the way – to the centers of consumption (e.g. to Central Europe). One of the key benefits claimed by the advocates of this concept is that because of the economies of scale to be expected, it is both technically efficient and cheaper than a decentralized expansion of renewable energies (Werner 2007). They also argue that the concept provides for greater efficiency in terms of system integration: a geographically spread out, combined system, they say, would make it easier to balance out intermittent electricity sources such as wind power – especially if solar thermal power stations were a part of this combined system. The contribution of the latter to system integration is seen above all in their ability to feed in electricity continually and reliably (by using special storage systems at night). It is expected that solar thermal power plants will be capable of providing guaranteed and stable capacities of base load and balancing power, thus making them an important component of a transformed (super) grid, which (at least in the long term) will be based predominantly on renewable energies. The vision of such a "supergrid" also entails a long-term restructuring of the European and Mediterranean power system that involves a combination of declining dependency on fossil fuel-based and nuclear base load energy and a centralized concept of power generation largely in line with the present electricity supply system. Eventually, this may lead to a far-reaching transformation of existing structures of production and producer profiles. Because of the structural affinities between such a "supergrid" and the traditional centralized electricity system, there is also the possibility of restructuring the system architecture in a limited way by bringing the old and the new into a new, convergent relation with one another, that is, a convergence between centralizing strategies in the camp of the renewables on the one hand, and the integration of renewable energy technologies by the established electricity industry on the other.

Such a development is already visible in the case of the "Dii consortium" (Dii: Desertec industrial initiative), founded in summer 2009, which is planning to build up large-scale solar and wind power capacity in the North African and Middle Eastern deserts. The Desertec project emerged from a network of scientists and politicians initiated in 2003 by the Club of Rome, the Hamburg Climate Protection Foundation, and the Jordanian National Energy Research Centre (NERC). In the intervening years, they have sought to gain support for their project by writing scientific reports, engaging in public relations, and lobbying political leaders in Europe, North Africa, and the Middle East (Knies *et al.* 2008). This network, which was initially strongly influenced by actors from civil society, formed the nucleus of the Dii consortium. However, at present Dii consists mainly of (partly large-scale) enterprises from Europe, the Middle East, and North Africa, including manufacturers of renewable energy technologies, as well as several large electric power companies from Germany (Eon and RWE), Italy (Enel), Spain (RED Eléctrica de Espana), and Algeria (Cevital) (Dii GmbH 2013).[5] Given its present make-up, it is not yet clear whether those involved in the initiative view the project primarily as a complementary innovation within the framework of the existing electricity system, (which is still based mainly on large-scale centralized power plants) or as the core element of a fundamental change in the system *per se*. Whatever the case may be, the ambitious Desertec vision has yet to overcome a range of serious obstacles.

The Desertec protagonists have two main aims. First, by 2050 they want to achieve 100 percent self-generated energy supply (or as close to this as possible) in the Middle East and North Africa (MENA) using electricity from renewable energy sources. Second, Dii seeks to gradually increase the volume of electricity transmitted between the MENA states and Europe: up to 900 TWh in 2050, mainly from south to north to cover about 16 percent of total electricity consumption in Europe in 2050 (Dii GmbH 2013: 16–17). The technological challenges of the transcontinental Desertec vision appear to be huge, but they are not impossible to overcome because the entire project will be based on existing and widely proven technologies (concentrated solar power plants, photovoltaic, wind turbines, high-voltage direct-current transmission lines). The most challenging task, however – given the sociopolitical and socioeconomic conditions prevailing in the participating MENA states – will presumably be to embed the Desertec strategy appropriately in its cultural and social context. Alongside the far-reaching – and still largely unpredictable – political unrest in nearly all the MENA states as a result of the so-called Arab Spring (see Bradley 2012), there are also a number of economic, political, and legislative challenges to be overcome by the Desertec protagonists. A case study on Algeria (Wuppertal Institute/ CREAD 2010) emphasizes that most of the country's politicians and administrators are only willing to participate in a transcontinental electricity supply infrastructure project as intended by Desertec if a number of preconditions are met:

1   Domestic consumption of the electricity produced by solar power plants or wind farms must have absolute priority, given the rapidly increasing demand for energy in Algeria. Export of renewable electricity will only be a supplementary option in the case of future surplus production.

2   The Algerian economy must benefit by the setting up of a domestic renewable energy industry and by an increasing domestic employment rate.

3   There must be a transfer of know-how and technology from Europe to Algeria (Wuppertal Institute/CREAD 2010: 47–9).

The authors of the Algerian case study also outline the numerous legislative and administrative hurdles that impede private investment – especially foreign investment – in the national energy supply system (e.g. restrictive licensing procedures for investments in power plants or power grids, insufficient incentives for investments in renewable energies) (Wuppertal Institute/CREAD 2010: 36–8). The Algerian case may be specific in certain respects; however, the long list of "must haves" that the protagonists of the Desertec strategy consider as indispensable with regard to MENA underlines the fact that the Algerian case is not a unique one. Most of the recommended measures and strategies are addressed to governments, ministries, or regulators in the MENA states. They include:

- Implementation of an appropriate regulatory framework for private investments in renewable energy projects in MENA (e.g. secure land access, regulated grid access, transparent permit granting procedures, existence of independent regulators, completion of power market reforms);
- Involving domestic entrepreneurs in renewable energy development;
- Implementation of sound policies for proper use of the grid infrastructure (e.g. regulation for the improved use of existing grids in MENA, long-term transmission rights to facilitate grid investments and to secure access to transnational power lines for renewable export projects);
- Dedicated governmental commitment to renewables as new technologies in MENA (e.g. definition of national renewable energy targets as a share of consumption); and
- Dedicated international commitment to a power system based on renewable energies (e.g. binding regional framework for renewable energy targets in MENA, stepwise convergence of national approaches to generating renewable energy, commitment to binding climate action targets in MENA) (Dii GmbH 2013: 10–11, 24–5).

COMPETING VISIONS OF THE ENERGY TRANSITION

It is no coincidence that several large European power companies are involved in the Dii consortium, insofar as the Desertec project conforms to their accustomed strategy of making high volume investments in centralized power plants and high-voltage large-scale transmission grids. However, there are also some representatives of NGOs, such as the Club of Rome and Greenpeace,[6] who support the vision of a transcontinental "green" electricity alliance as well. Thus, the debate on (total) decentralization versus (at least partial) centralization of renewables' power supply has already led to a split among the proponents of renewable energies. In technical terms, two distinct solutions are in competition with one another: the "supergrid" solution is aimed at upgrading the grid infrastructure, especially by enhancing transnational and transcontinental transmission lines and networks, whereas the protagonists of a decentralized solution seek to downgrade the interregional grid infrastructure in order to free themselves from dependency on large grids and their operators (who are generally part of the incumbent power supply regime). However, this is not only a clash of controversial technological concepts, but also a confrontation between divergent sociopolitical objectives. The advocates of the "supergrid" regard their far-reaching vision in the first instance as being legitimated by its (energetic and economic) efficiency, which, in their view, the Desertec strategy can achieve.[7] They believe that the path of pure decentralization will lead to a tremendous waste of energy, insofar as it is dependent on a multitude of (in some cases) inefficient power sources (e.g. small photovoltaic panels on householders' rooftops) and more or less inefficient storage technologies.[8] In addition to the efficiency issue, the "supergrid" protagonists emphasize the socioeconomic benefits, which they claim will accrue to the participating countries, especially in the MENA region. Thus, the editors of *Desert Power: Getting Started*[9] state that "large markets for renewables in the MENA region provide an opportunity for local value creation. At the same time, creating local employment is a crucial argument – and even a prerequisite – for government commitment to renewables in many MENA countries" (Dii GmbH 2013: 13).

In contrast to this, the protagonists of far-reaching decentralization of the energy system see their goals legitimated first and foremost by the expected "democratization" of power supply. They are concerned to achieve energy autonomy, as indicated most clearly in the work of Hermann Scheer (e.g. 2006, 2012), one of the most distinguished proponents of a transition towards decentralized renewable energies until his death in 2010. Energy autonomy means overcoming heteronomous – or "undemocratic" – forms of energy supply that go hand-in-hand with a lack of freedom to reach autonomous decisions and opportunities for action on the part of energy consumers. According-ing to Scheer (2012), a comprehensive energy transition towards renewables is only possible if a multitude of decentralized bottom–up actors gain control over renewable energy sources and free themselves from the pressures and restrictions imposed by the still dominant cap-italist, shareholder value-driven energy companies, which are clearly not interested in departing from their traditional technological path of centralized nuclear and coal-fired power plants. Overcoming these outdated but still dominant structures demands the empowerment of citizens, NGOs, community energy initiatives, municipalities, local utilities, and start-ups in the renewables sector, as well as an intensifi-cation of existing activities (see Chapter 4). This vision of sociotechni-cal decentralization is aimed at increasing the extent to which local communities or regions can supply themselves with electricity (using private solar panels, citizen-owned power plants, publicly-owned wind farms, etc.), heat (using CHP plants at a district level), and bio-fuels (using regional biomass sources). Therefore, the advocates of energy-related decentralization and democratization are simultane-ously keen to influence regional and agricultural policies.

These arguments indicate clearly that there is a clash between two sociotechnical visions whose programs cannot easily be reconciled. Even if we were to consider a combined – centralized–decentralized – solution, the demands on processes of governance in terms of energy policy would increase dramatically. The idea of decentralization requires completely different political measures, criteria for funding, and processes of coordination among all those involved than the con-cept of transnational centralization combined with a cross-linkage to renewable sources of power generation. These opposing targets would have to be reconciled not only by integrating the two visions, but also by developing an integrated – and internationally coordinated – political concept. Whereas a further decentralization of power generation would follow an already established path in some countries (such as Denmark, Germany, or Austria) and could build on existing potential in terms of technologies and actors in the renewable energy sector, the concept of a "supergrid" is something altogether different. At present, it could build on the hitherto dominant system logic as well as on the increasing number of huge offshore wind farms, particularly in the United Kingdom and Scandinavia, and on numerous large onshore wind farms, for example in Spain or North Germany. However, the "supergrid" vision would still require the internationally coordinated construction of a gigantic infrastructure – not only in the MENA states – and, furthermore, would have to face the problem that the new construction of transmission lines is quite difficult in most European countries today. The main reason for this is a low level of acceptance on the part of the population, prompting the risk of local resistance, legal rows, and lengthy approval procedures.

With this potential for conflict in mind, it bears asking whether or not the process of integrating renewable energies into the overall energy supply system, which began some time ago, will ultimately lead to a confrontation between incompatible strands of development. If we rule out the possibility of long-term system instability, does that translate into a political and economic imperative to set a fixed course for the energy sector? If this were so, due to the need for compatibility, it would almost certainly lead either to a far-reaching substitution of the centralized power plant structures by decentralized renewable energies, or to a reformed and restabilized variant of the centralized electricity system. In either case, the emergence of a new "dominant design" – the outcome of a complex real-world experiment – would require sizeable structural change in the existing electricity system. To be sure, the decentralized option can move ahead smoothly on the basis of existing niche dynamics in some European countries, but it would still require fundamental change in the present stock of conventional power plants, as well as a change of business strategy and organizational structure on the part of the electric power companies (e.g. a radical reduction of coal-fired and

nuclear power plants, a switch to decentralized gas-fired power stations, and accelerated entry into renewable energies). By contrast, the
centralized option would – considering targets relating to international climate change policy – require the electric power companies
to quickly switch to plant technologies that generate fewer CO_2
emissions (gas-fired power plants, carbon capture and storage, large-
scale renewable energy plants). It would also require a profound
change in direction on the part of the renewable energy industry
towards large-scale technologies and projects. As far as we can see,
system integration is still at the stage of sociotechnical "fermentation," a
stage that is marked by considerable uncertainty – not only regarding
the future breakthrough of a new "dominant design," but also in
terms of the socioeconomic drivers and power relations that will ultimately set the direction of energy transition as we go forward.

TOWARDS A TRANSFORMATION OF THE
ELECTRICITY SECTOR

Since the rediscovery of renewable energies in the 1970s, many electricity systems all over the world have passed through transformation processes that can be described as a confrontation between
competing sociotechnical paradigms. In the course of this confrontation, renewables have become a serious challenge for more traditionally organized electricity sectors. Pioneer countries in renewable
energy utilization (e.g. Denmark and Germany) have formulated the
fundamental principles of the new paradigm, namely decentralized
energy production, pluralized participation, and environmental and
climate protection. As such, they have chosen deliberately to disso-
ciate from the previously existing energy system. The development
of decentralized governance structures that included a wide range of
NGOs and citizen groups, ongoing government support, a supportive legal framework, and (in part) a system of close consultation
between the operators of renewable power plants and the plant manufacturers were the key reasons for the rapid development of niche
dynamics and the early dissemination of renewable energies.

Despite the remarkable expansion of the renewable energy industry in recent years, the traditional electricity sector still remains the

dominant economic and technological force in the field of power generation and distribution. It continues to display a set of strategies that are aimed at restabilizing the traditional centralized energy system and preserving it over the long term – the participation of several large (mostly European) energy companies in large-scale offshore wind farms, as well as in the transcontinental Desertec project, can be seen as one core element of this strategy. Moreover, the protagonists of renewable energies find themselves consistently confronted with new challenges, as the previously well-defined profile of the new sociotechnical paradigm has become much less clear-cut. There are at least two main reasons for this. First, the expansion of renewable power generation frequently provokes local or regional conflicts due to a lack of acceptance by local people, often on the basis of expected environmental harm and/or a perceived threat to their quality of life. This often leads to outright opposition by people living in close proximity to wind farms or outdoor solar energy plants and additionally gives rise to conflicts within the ranks of the environmental movement itself. Second, with the increasing amount of "green" electricity coming on stream, it has become more and more clear that any future expansion or sought-after dominance of a renewable power supply will only be achieved if the protagonists of renewable energy themselves succeed in establishing a better integration of renewable power sources into the overall system, and do not leave this task to the incumbent electricity suppliers.

As a new "dominant design" has not yet emerged, the transformation of the energy sector is still in a phase of "fermentation" and experimentation – with all the risks and opportunities entailed by such a phase. As a result, there is more than one option available for the further development of renewable energies. On the one hand, this openness could provide fresh impetus for the expansion of renewable energies by attracting a wide range of actors to this environmentally *and* economically key sector (for instance, institutional investors, innovative companies, municipalities, utilities, energy cooperatives, citizen groups). On the other hand, it might serve to reinforce an already perceptible tendency towards disagreement within the renewables sector regarding, for example, the problem of system integration and whether a more centralized or a rigorously decentralized mode of diffusion should be preferred.

NOTES

1 A pioneering German example of a combined renewable power plant is discussed in Rohrig (2010).

2 For a global overview of so-called "power to gas" demonstration projects, see Iskov and Rasmussen (2013). For a description of an autonomous wind/hydro energy demonstration system located on the Norwegian island of Utsira, see Ulleberg *et al.* (2010). For an overview and a description of all current German "power to gas" projects in operation, under construction, or at the planning stage, see Strategieplattform Power to Gas (www.powertogas.info). Accessed March 1, 2014.

3 In the case of "power to hydrogen to power," the efficiency factor ranges between 34 percent and 44 percent (Sterner and Jentsch 2011).

4 With regard to "power to gas," see again the overview provided by Iskov and Rasmussen (2013) and the various technological solutions they describe.

5 As of December 2013 Dii comprises 19 shareholders and 17 associated partners. It also has consultative relations with 11 national or regional institutions and organizations of the MENA states (MENA: Middle East – North Africa); www.dii-eumena.com/about-us/network.html (accessed December 1, 2013).

6 See Werner (2007) and his appeal for a "supergrid" to support the expansion of energy supply by renewables. Robert Werner is a former chairman of Greenpeace Energy.

7 See Dii GmbH (2012). The efficiency issue is a common thread that runs through the Dii report on "The Case for Desert Power."

8 Any process of energy conversion and storage will be accompanied by energy losses. For an example, see the previously mentioned case of "power to gas and gas to power."

9 *Desert Power: Getting Started* was published by Dii GmbH in 2013 as "the manual for renewable electricity in MENA." The report "proposes pragmatic first steps towards sustainable and affordable electricity" for MENA and Europe "and also presents a private-sector perspective on the Mediterranean Solar Plan" (Dii GmbH 2013: 3).

9

CONCLUSION

NONKNOWLEDGE
AND EXNOVATION
AS PROGRESS

As more and more novel technologies are developed for utilizing renewable energy sources above and below the Earth's crust, the boundary between science and the everyday world of human beings is becoming increasingly blurred. Whereas the specialized world of scientific institutions has traditionally allowed scientists alone to do experimental research and propose theoretical explanations for worldly phenomena, research on energy has increasingly turned society into a laboratory – one in which the energy user and non-scientist can potentially play an active part in the experiment, be it via civil society engagement, novel forms of public participation, energy cooperatives, or social networks. This new "society as laboratory" context is characterized by an extraordinary degree of complexity in terms of both the range and number of actors involved and the framework conditions that govern the real-world experiments taking place there. Thus, in many respects energy transition means acting under conditions of uncertainty and unpredictability: those involved in developing and using renewable energy technologies inevitably have to be prepared to deal with the unintended outcomes of their actions, and these – by definition – cannot be anticipated precisely, if at all. For example, using novel forms of public participation appears inevitable, but can be a risky process as well – any far-reaching decentralization of power generation will require the involvement of individuals and households, as well as the mobilization of civil society groups. However, it is extremely hard to predict the extent to which energy consumers will be able or willing to change their previously "unthinking" patterns of energy consumption and start using and generating electricity at a household level as a high interest product. Similarly, the active involvement of civil society groups may well help to speed up and intensify the transition towards renewable energy use, and yet at the same time it might also motivate civil society opponents of decentralized renewable energy projects to redouble their efforts to prevent the construction of regional wind farms, local geothermal power plants, large solar power plants, and similar energy facilities. Whenever such divergent interests clash, there is bound to be considerable uncertainty regarding the outcomes.

More generally speaking, what is at issue here is the inherent contingency that characterizes networks of local and regional actors – not only with regard to conflicts around specific renewable energy projects, but also in terms of the interactions that occur between lay proponents of renewable energies and policy makers. This is all the more true when we consider the multitude of stakeholders involved – utilities, energy companies, grid operators, manufacturers and operators of renewable energy technologies, suppliers, farmers, homeowners, unions, NGOs, to name just a few. Each of these will seek to communicate their own interests and objectives to the political representatives concerned, not only at local or regional level but also at national and even transnational level. Last, but not least, we have seen that even among the proponents of renewable energies there are competing visions and sociotechnical objectives, not least over the issue of a decentralized versus (at least in part) centralized energy transition pathway. This entails considerable uncertainty over whether a new "dominant design" will emerge out of the present phase of technological "fermentation." Thus, the chances of anticipating future developments in (global) energy transition along with its broader economic, socio-technical, and sociocultural consequences are rather limited. These limitations also apply to transition theory (see Chapter 3). The specific strengths of transition theory, as described in Chapter 3, comprise, in particular, the (historical) reconstruction and detailed analysis of already accomplished transition processes, for example, the analysis of multifaceted interrelations between niche innovations, landscape pressures, and regime change and the mechanisms by which niche developments are taken up into existing sociotechnical regimes. Moreover, transition theory can also provide a helpful framework for studying current processes of sociotechnical change and for formu-lating plausible assumptions about possible outcomes. However, when it comes to predicting the ultimate outcomes of such – often lengthy – transition periods, we prefer to follow the approach taken by Frank Laird (2013) who states that "changes in energy systems [interact] with myriad social, political, and cultural features of soci-ety." He criticizes ideas that "are based on a simplistic relationship of energy to society," insofar as they ignore "the idea that different societies can arise from similar material bases and that social changes that follow changes to technological systems are impossible to predict" (Laird 2013: 153–4). Whereas this view runs contrary to some of Max Weber's reflections on the role of natural resources in the rise of capitalism (Chapter 2), it resonates well with Vaclav Smil's (2010) observation that energy transitions are a complex and incremental process in which explicit attempts to quickly change established forms of energy utilization are doomed to failure.

In addition, it begins to appear reasonable to conjecture that the experimental nature of the recursive design processes we have observed in many areas of renewable energy production has not necessarily been a sign of technology development in its early stages or of an irresponsible tinkering with sociotechnical artifacts, but is actually an essential feature of technological innovation. We have observed that the consultation processes between practitioners and researchers in the field of renewable energy are continually enriched by the ongoing discovery of new technical options, new risks, and knowledge gaps, as well as technological uncertainties and behavioral and organiza-tional contingencies. Thus, it is erroneous to regard ignorance merely as a factor that exists at the early stages of a research project or a technological test case; instead, it appears more appropriate to regard it as an inevitable (and possibly necessary) component of such processes, one that needs to be produced, refined, and – perhaps most importantly – acknowledged by the actors involved so that the ensuing nonknowledge can be rendered useful for developing novel forms of energy technology.

In contrast to approaches that externalize ignorance and nonknowledge by analyzing risk assessments or those that sidestep it by using rhetorics of certainty, the cases of renewable energy transition we have discussed so far suggest that the unexpected aspects of knowledge production can be analyzed effectively using the notion of experimentality. In the course of this, nonknowledge is not devalued as a regrettable shortcoming, but is instead seen as a useful means to reach responsible decisions in situations of unavoidable risk and ambiguity. After all, if the acceleration of knowledge production in the twenty-first century has indeed constructed more areas of ignorance and has therefore paradoxically made mishaps and failures more likely, then society needs to find creative and innovative solutions to cope with the increase in knowledge gaps that arise in this way. This is important given that calls for greater certainty and safety are being heard ever more loudly in contemporary political debates on energy issues. At the same time, empirical research on decision making in real-world cases has revealed an increase in "experimentalities" as a reaction to unavoidable uncertainty and ignorance, that is, a response to modernist beliefs in scientific certainty. This resonates with observations made by Brian Wynne (2005) regarding different types of complexity and limits of predictability, which are readily apparent within different genomics research and practitioner cultures and yet largely denied by the scientists themselves. Thus, perhaps the experimental strategies observed in real-world decision making are indicative of a change in practical ways of coping with uncertainty and ignorance – even if the official rhetorics still suggest otherwise.

In order to pursue successful strategies of energy transition in modern societies, it would therefore appear to be crucial not only to discuss issues around public acceptance of novel technologies, but, more importantly, to integrate processes of learning from mishaps at an institutional level so that unforeseen risks and nonknowledge are handled in a socially responsible way. This, of course, is no easy task. Many developments that have occurred in the course of establishing the use of renewable energies have more often than not been a random or even accidental outcome of the real-world experiments discussed throughout this book. Equally, however, no new (or reformed) sociotechnical regime can be established by simply trying to convince the public of its importance. Calls for greater public participation and for the democratization of science in general indicate that this is widely recognized. This point is even more crucial given that, in many experimental design processes, it is not even possible to undertake any accurate risk assessment. Such processes simply elude frameworks of risk assessment because there is not enough experiential data to rely on for evaluating future events in any meaningful way. In this sense, there are good reasons for opposing experimental processes in the transition towards renewable energy. Yet, in view of the inevitable ignorance involved in any novel form of technology and the fact that doing nothing (e.g. moving further down the road paved with coal, oil, or nuclear power) may be the worst decision to take, the risks of adopting an experimental mode to shape future energy supply may prove to be the least intimidating.

Needless to say, a willingness to acknowledge nonknowledge when developing new solutions will always go hand-in-hand with generating yet more ignorance. As we have seen, the turn towards renewable sources of energy has been accompanied by an intensification of sociopolitical negotiations around a variety of related issues. These include technoscientific questions regarding the relationship between old and new technologies, organizational questions to do with the centralization or decentralization of relevant structures, and issues around stakeholder involvement and the role of political and social movements. What these increasingly public processes of negotiation suggest is that a new mode of knowledge production is in the making, one that bears all the hallmarks of transdisciplinarity in its broadest sense (Blumer *et al.* 2013, Nowotny *et al.* 2001, Pohl and Hirsch Hadorn 2007). When viewed in this context, transdisciplinary processes can be seen to reflect a broad shift in society that effectively blurs the distinction between scientific knowledge and knowledge produced outside the realm of science. Real-world experiments involving the application of knowledge and the subsequent discovery of ever more nonknowledge can, therefore, be regarded as an institutional mechanism that is potentially capable of enhancing symbolic power and making it easier for scientific activities to become legitimized in the wider – experimental – society. Furthermore, recent observations regarding the increase in collaborations between artists and ecologists (Ingram 2012), art–science pedagogy (Born and Barry 2010), and even fusions between aesthetic and scientific methods (Edwards 2008) indicate that this age of post-normal science (Ravetz 2012) in the experimental society is a multifaceted one. This suggests further that knowledge about developing new energy sources is nowadays produced in the course of applying that same knowledge in a process in which heterogeneous actors come together in hybrid groups to cope in collaborative fashion with inevitable uncertainty and risk. Given that scientific debate is always focused on statements based on varying amounts of nonknowledge, developing creative strategies to deal with this is of upmost importance. In his discussion of green nanotechnology, Colin Milburn (2012) has argued that successful cooperation between environmental policy makers and proponents of green nanopolitics may best be understood in terms of practicing science fiction in the real world. To start from this point – to acknowledge the experimental nature of our transition towards renewable energies and, in doing so, to conceptualize associated practices in new ways – appears to offer exciting options in our quest to understand the widely proclaimed energy transition in many countries from a sociological perspective. It also offers an opportunity to build theory and to devise pragmatic policy strategies for dealing successfully with inevitable and sometimes even very useful surprises. In this sense, new knowledge is generating new practical options, albeit without providing any clear criteria or ready-made expertise for deciding how they should be handled. Particularly fascinating is the way in which many engineers and scientists – in contrast to popular notions of scientific objectivity and reliable technical expertise – are noticeably making use of supposedly outdated and non-rational tools (open curiosity, trust in chance, "old" technology, failure as a normal stepping stone) to advance the generation of renewable energy in an allegedly hi-tech and rational world.

Finally, a concluding remark on the seeming opposition between novelty and the apparent "shock of the old" (Edgerton 2007) may be in order. Whereas the contemporary phase of transition towards renewable energy sources may appear to be just one more transition among many others, it should be abundantly apparent that it is not. Although societies all over the world have moved from using human muscle power to domesticating animals, inventing agricultural methods, exploiting fossil resources such as coal, gas, and oil, and, most recently, harnessing nuclear power, the current transition is one in which we cannot simply add yet another energy source to the existing ones. Instead, we will need to "exnovate" existing forms of energy utilization in order to get rid of outdated technologies and forms of energy usage. The age of renewable resources is very likely to still include energy from human and animal muscles and from plants and crops; however, in order to eliminate existing unsustainable modes of energy utilization and technology development, a gradual process of exnovation will inevitably be required that is almost certain to herald the end – sooner or later – of the fossil fuel phase and perhaps also of the nuclear phase.

References

Adams, R. N., 1975. *Energy and Structure: A Theory of Social Power.* Austin, TX: University of Texas Press.

Ahrweiler, P. and Keane, M. T., 2013. Innovation Networks. *Mind & Society*, 12 (1), 73–90.

Akrich, M., 1993. A Gazogene in Costa Rica: An Experiment in Techno-Sociology. *In*: Lemmonier, P., ed. *Technological Choices: Transformation in Material Cultures since the Neolithic.* London: Routledge, 289–337.

Ancygier, A., Bah, I., Renzig, S., Wandler, R. and Zimmermann, J. R., 2013. EEG: Ein Modell für Europa? *Neue Energie*, 5, 20–35.

Ansell, C., 2012. What is a "Democratic Experiment"? *Contemporary Pragmatism*, 9 (2), 159–80.

Bakewell, S., 2012. Largest Offshore Wind Farm Generates First Power in U.K. Bloomberg. *Renewable Energy.World.Com*. Available from: www.renewableenergyworld.com/rea/news/article/2012/10/largest-offshore-wind-farm-generates-first-power-in-u-k (accessed May 19, 2013).

Bartiaux, F. and Salmón, L. R., 2014. Family Dynamics and Social Practice Theories: An Investigation of Daily Practices Related to Food, Mobility, Energy Consumption and Tourism. *Nature + Culture*, 9 (2), 204–24.

Bauknecht, D. and Voß, J. P., 2009. Network Regulation. *In*: Praetorius, B., ed. *Innovation for Sustainable Electricity Systems. Exploring the Dynamics of Energy Transitions.* Heidelberg, Germany: Physica, 191–226.

Beisel, U. and Schneider, T., 2012. Provincialising Waste: The Transformation of Ambulance car 7/83-2 to tro-tro Dr Jesus. *Environment and Planning D: Society and Space*, 30 (4), 639–54.

Bensmann, M., 2007. Freie Fahrt für Fermenter. *Neue Energie*, 1, 52–5.

Björnsson, S., 2010. *Geothermal Development and Research in Iceland*. Reykjavik, Orkustofnun. Available from: www.nea.is/media/utgafa/GD_loka.pdf (accessed March 1, 2014).

Blättel-Mink, B. and Hellmann, K. -U., eds., 2010. *Prosumer Revisited: Zur Aktualität einer Debatte*. Wiesbaden, Germany: VS Verlag.

Bloomquist, G., Lund, J. and Gehringer, M., 2013. Geothermal Energy. *In*: Crawley, G.M., ed. *The World Scientific Handbook of Energy*. Hackensack, NJ: World Scientific Publishing, 245–73.

Blumer, Y. B., Stauffacher, M., Lang, D. J., Hayashic, K. and Uchidac, S., 2013. Non-technical Success Factors for Bioenergy Projects: Learning from a Multiple Case Study in Japan. *Energy Policy*, 60, 386–95.

Blumler, M. A., 2008. The Fossil Fuel Revolution: A Great, and Largely Unrecognized, Experiment. *Pennsylvania Geographer*, 46 (2), 3–21.

BMU (Bundesministerium für Umwelt, Naturschutz und Reaktorsicherheit), 2005. *Umwelt macht Arbeit*. Das Wirtschaftsmagazin des Bundesumweltministeriums. Berlin, Germany: BMU.

BMU (Bundesministerium für Umwelt, Naturschutz und Reaktorsicherheit), 2012. *Erneuerbare Energien in Zahlen. Nationale und internationale Entwicklung*. Berlin, Germany: BMU.

BMU (Federal Ministry for the Environment, Nature Conservation and Nuclear Safety), ed., 2013a. *Renewable Energies in Figures*. National and International Development. Berlin, Germany: BMU.

BMU (Bundesministerium für Umwelt, Naturschutz und Reaktorsicherheit), ed., 2013b. Offshore-Windenergie. Ein Überblick über die Aktivitäten in Deutschland. Berlin, Germany: BMU.

BMWi/BMU (Bundesministerium für Wirtschaft und Technologie/Bundesministerium für Umwelt, Naturschutz und Reaktorsicherheit), eds., 2010. *Energiekonzept für eine umweltschonende, zuverlässige und bezahlbare Energieversorgung*. Berlin, Germany: BMWi/BMU.

Born, G. and Barry, A., 2010. Art–Science: From Public Understanding to Public Experiment. *Journal of Cultural Economy*, 3 (1), 103–19.

Böschen, S., 2009. Hybrid Regimes of Knowledge? Challenges for Constructing Scientific Evidence in the Context of the GMO Debate. *Environmental Science and Pollution Research*, 16 (5), 508–20.

Böschen, S., 2013. Modes of Constructing Evidence: Sustainable Development as Social Experimentation – The Cases of Chemical Regulations and Climate Change Politics. *Nature + Culture*, 8 (1), 74–96.

Bovet, J. and Köck, W., 2012. Zur Zulässigkeit von Kleinwindanlagen in reinen Wohngebieten. *Neue Zeitschrift für Verwaltungsrecht*, 31 (2), 153–8.

Bradley, J. R., 2012. *After the Arab Spring: How Islamists Hijacked the Middle East Revolts*. Houndmills, UK: Palgrave Macmillan.

Brand, K. -W., 2010. Social Practices and Sustainable Consumption: Benefits and Limitations of a New Theoretical Approach. *In*: Gross, M. and H. Heinrichs, eds, *Environmental Sociology: European Perspectives and Interdisciplinary Challenges*. Dordrecht, Netherlands: Springer, 217–35.

Braun-Thürmann, H., 2005. *Innovation*. Bielefeld, Germany: Transcript.

Breslau, D., 2013. Studying and Doing Energy Transition. *Nature + Culture*, 8 (3), 324–30.

Brock, B., 2010. Cheerful and Heroic Failure. *In*: Le Feuvre, L., ed. *Failure: Documents of Contemporary Art*. Cambridge, MA: MIT Press, 180–2.

Bühl, W. L., 1980. Das ökologische Paradigma in der Soziologie. *In*: Niemeyer, H., ed. *Soziale Beziehungsgeflechte*. Berlin, Germany: Duncker & Humblot, 97–122.

Butler, C., Parkhill, K. and Pidgeon, N., 2013. Nuclear Power after 3/11: Looking Back and Thinking Ahead. *In*: Hindmarsh, R., ed. *Nuclear Disaster at Fukushima Daiichi: Social, Political and Environmental Issues*. London: Routledge, 135–53.

Buttel, F. H., 1978. Social Structure and Energy Efficiency: A Preliminary Cross-National Analysis. *Human Ecology*, 6 (2), 145–64.

Byzio, A. and Mautz, R., 2006. Offshore-Windkraftnutzung im Spannungsfeld von institutioneller Einbettung, Risikodiskurs und Konfliktdynamik. *In*: Heine, H., M. Schumann and V. Wittke, eds. *Wer den Ast absägt, auf dem er sitzt, kann deshalb noch längst nicht fliegen. Innovationen zwischen institutionellem Wandel und Pfadkontinuitäten*. Berlin, Germany: Sigma, 64–83.

Byzio, A., Mautz, R. and Rosenbaum, W., 2005. *Energiewende in schwerer See? Konflikte um die Offshore-Windkraftnutzung*. Munich, Germany: Oekom.

Campbell, D. T., 1998. The Experimenting Society. *In*: Dunn, W. N., ed. *The Experimenting Society: Essays in Honor of Donald T. Campbell*. New Brunswick, NJ: Transaction Publishers, 35–68.

Canan, P., 1986. Rethinking Geothermal Energy's Contribution to Community Development. *Geothermics*, 15 (4), 431–4.

Castells, M., 1996. *The Rise of the Network Society – The Information Age: Economy, Society and Culture Vol. I.* Oxford, UK: Blackwell.

Catton, W. R. and Dunlap, R., 1978. Environmental Sociology: A New Paradigm. *The American Sociologist*, 13 (1), 41–9.

Commoner, B., 1971. *The Closing Circle: Nature, Man, and Technology.* New York, NY: Knopf.

Cottrell, F., 1955. *Energy and Society: The Relation between Energy, Social Change, and Economic Development.* New York, NY: McGraw-Hill.

Cottrell, F., 2009. *Energy and Society (Revised). The Relation between Energy, Social Change, and Economic Development.* Bloomington, IN: Author House.

de Laet, M. and Mol, A., 2000. The Zimbabwe Bush Pump: Mechanics of a Fluid Technology. *Social Studies of Science*, 30 (2), 225–63.

Dean, D. R., 1992. *James Hutton and the History of Geology.* Ithaca, NY: Cornell University Press.

DeGunther, R., 2009. *Alternative Energy for Dummies.* New York, NY: John Wiley & Sons.

Dehnhardt, A. and Petschow, U., 2004. Nobody is perfect! Erneuerbare Energien, externe Effekte und ökonomische Bewertung. *Ökologisches Wirtschaften*, 5, 24–5.

Devine-Wright, P. and Howes, Y., 2010. Disruption to Place Attachment and the Protection of Restorative Environments: A Wind Energy Case Study. *Journal of Environmental Psychology*, 30 (3), 271–80.

Dii GmbH, ed., 2012. 2050 – *Desert Power: The Case for Desert Power.* Munich, Germany: Executive Summary Dii GmbH.

Dii GmbH, ed., 2013. *Desert Power: Getting Started. The Manual for Renewable Electricity in MENA.* Munich, Germany: Executive Summary Dii GmbH.

Dolata, U., 2013. *The Transformative Capacity of New Technologies: A Theory of Sociotechnical Change.* London: Routledge.

Dolata, U. and Werle, R., 2007. "Bringing technology back in": Technik als Einflussfaktor sozioökonomischen und institutionellen Wandels. *In*: Dolata, U. and R. Werle, eds. *Gesellschaft und die Macht der Technik: Sozioökonomischer und institutioneller Wandel durch Technisierung.* Frankfurt am Main: Campus Verlag, 15–43.

Dosi, G., 1982. Technological Paradigms and Technological Trajectories: A Suggested Interpretation of the Determinants and Directions of Technical Change. *Research Policy*, 11 (3), 147–62.

Dowd, A. M., Boughen, N., Ashworth, P. and Carr-Cornish, S., 2011. Geothermal Technology in Australia: Investigating Social Acceptance. *Energy Policy*, 39 (10), 6301–7.

Dunlap, R., 2011. Aktuelle Entwicklungen in der nordamerikanischen Umweltsoziologie. *In*: Gross, M., ed. *Handbuch Umweltsoziologie*. Wiesbaden, Germany: Springer, 54–72.

Durkheim, E., 1933 [1893]. *The Division of Labor in Society*. Glencoe, IL: Free Press.

Durkheim, E., 1947 [1912]. *The Elementary Forms of Religious Life*. Glencoe, IL: Free Press.

Edelstein, M. R. and Kleese, D. A., 1995. Cultural Relativity of Impact Assessment: Native Hawaiian Opposition to Geothermal Energy Development. *Society & Natural Resources*, 8 (1), 19–31.

Edgerton, D., 2007. *The Shock of the Old: Technology and Global History since 1900*. Oxford, UK: Oxford University Press.

Edwards, D., 2008. *Artscience: Creativity in the Post-Google Generation*. Cambridge, MA: Harvard University Press.

Eglash, R., Croissant, J. L., Di Chiro, G. and Fouché, R., eds., 2004. *Appropriating Technology: Vernacular Science and Social Power*. Minneapolis, MN: University of Minnesota Press.

Eichhorn, M. and Drechsler, M., 2010. Spatial Trade-offs Between Wind Power Production and Bird Collision Avoidance in Agricultural Landscapes. *Ecology and Society*, 15 (2), art. 10.

Ellul, J., 1964. *The Technological Society*. New York, NY: Alfred Knopf.

Evans, A. B., 2005. Jules Verne: Exploring the Limits. *Australian Journal of French Studies*, 42 (3), 265–75.

EWEA (The European Wind Energy Association), 2005. *Large Scale Integration of Wind Energy in the European Power Supply: Analysis, Issues and Recommendations*. Brussels: EWEA.

EWEA (The European Wind Energy Association), ed., 2013. *The European offshore wind industry – key trends and statistics 2012*. Brussels: EWEA.

Ferguson, E. S., 1992. *Engineering and the Mind's Eye*. Cambridge, MA: MIT Press.

Finger, J. and Blankenship, D., 2010. *Handbook of Best Practices for Geothermal Drilling*. Albuquerque, NM: Sandia National Laboratories. Sandia Report SAND2010-6048.

Firestein, S., 2012. *Ignorance: How it Drives Science*. Oxford, UK: Oxford University Press.

Foster, J. B. and Holleman, H., 2012. Weber and the Environment: Classical Foundations for a Postexemptionalist Sociology. *American Journal of Sociology*, 117 (6), 1625–73.

Fox, D. B., Sutter, D. and Tester, J. W., 2011. The Thermal Spectrum of Low-Temperature Energy Use in the United States. *Energy & Environmental Science*, 4 (10), 3731–40.

Freeman, C. and Perez, C., 1988. Structural Crisis of Adjustment, Business Cycles and Investment Behaviour. *In*: Dosi, G., C. Freeman, R. Nelson, G. Silverberg and L. Soete, eds. *Technical Change and Economic Theory*. London: Pinter, 38–66.

Frei, C., 2013. Assessing the Global Energy Agenda. *In*: World Energy Council, ed. *2013 World Energy Issues Monitor*. London: World Energy Council, 5–8.

Frick, S., Van Wees, J., Kaltschmitt, M. and Schröder, G., 2010. Economic Performance and Environmental Assessment. *In*: Huenges, E., ed. *Geothermal Energy Systems: Exploration, Development, and Utilization*. Weinheim, Germany: Wiley, 373–421.

Fuchs, G. and Wassermann, S., 2012. From Niche to Mass Markets in High Technology: The Case of Photovoltaics in Germany. *In*: Bauer, J., A. Lang, and V. Schneider, eds. *Innovation Policy and Governance in High-Tech Industries: The Complexity of Coordination*. Heidelberg, Germany: Springer, 219–44.

Fücks, R., 2013. *Intelligent wachsen: Die grüne Revolution*. München, Germany: Hanser.

Garud, R. and Karnøe, P., 2003. Bricolage versus Breakthrough: Distributed and Embedded Agency in Technology Entrepreneurship. *Research Policy*, 32 (2), 277–300.

Gawel, E., Strunz, S. and Lehmann, P., 2013. Germany's Energy Transition under Attack: Is There an Inscrutable German *Sonderweg*? *Nature + Culture*, 8 (2), 121–33.

Geels, F. W., 2002. Technological Transitions as Evolutionary Reconfiguration Processes: A Multi-level Perspective and a Case-study. *Research Policy*, 31 (8–9), 1257–74.

Geels, F. W., 2004. From Sectoral Systems of Innovations to Socio-technical Systems: Insights about Dynamics and Change from Sociology and Institutional Theory. *Research Policy*, 33 (6–7), 897–920.

Geels, F. W., 2005. *Technological Transitions and System Innovations. A Co-Evolutionary and Socio-Technical Analysis*. Cheltenham, UK: Elgar.

Geels, F. W., 2010. Ontologies, Socio-technical Transitions (to Sustainability), and the Multi-level Perspective. *Research Policy*, 39 (4), 495–510.

Geels, F. W. and Schot, J., 2007. Typology of Sociotechnical Transition Pathways. *Research Policy*, 36 (3), 399–417.

Geels, F. W. and Schot, J., 2010. The Dynamics of Transitions: A Socio-Technical Perspective. *In*: Grin, J., J. Rotmans and J. Schot, eds. *Transitions to Sustainable Development: New Directions in the Study of Long Term Transformative Change*. London: Routledge, 11–101.

Georgescu-Roegen, N., 1971. *The Entropy Law and the Economic Process*. Cambridge, MA: Harvard University Press.

Giardini, D., 2009. Geothermal Quake Risks must be Faced. *Nature*, 462, 848–9.

Gilfillan, S. C., 1970 [1935]. *The Sociology of Invention*. Cambridge, MA: MIT Press.

Glassley, W. E., 2010. *Geothermal Energy: Renewable Energy and the Environment*. London: CRC Press.

Goffman, E., 1967. *Interaction Ritual: Essays in Face-to-face Behavior*. New York, NY: Doubleday.

Grau, T., Huo, M. and Neuhoff, K., 2012. Survey of Photovoltaic Industry and Policy in Germany and China. *Energy Policy*, 51 (1), 20–37.

Greene, M. T., 1983. *Geology in the Nineteenth Century: Changing View of a Changing World*. Ithaca, NY: Cornell University Press.

Grin, J., Rotmans, J. and Schot, J., 2010. *Transitions to Sustainable Development. New Directions in the Study of Long Term Transformative Change*. London: Routledge.

Gross, M., 2001. *Die Natur der Gesellschaft: Eine Geschichte der Umweltsoziologie*. Weinheim, Germany: Juventa Verlag.

Gross, M., 2003. *Inventing Nature: Ecological Restoration by Public Experiments*. Lanham, MD: Lexington Books.

Gross, M., 2010a. *Ignorance and Surprise: Science, Society, and Ecological Design*. Cambridge, MA: MIT Press.

Gross, M., 2010b. Social and Ecological Control: Ross's Early Contribution. *In*: Chriss, J., ed. *Social Control: Informal, Legal and Medical*. Bingley, UK: Emerald, 91–107.

Gross, M., 2012. Objective Culture and the Development of Nonknowledge: Georg Simmel and the Reverse Side of Knowing. *Cultural Sociology*, 6 (4) 422–37.

Gross, M., 2013. Old Science Fiction, New Inspiration: Communicating Unknowns in the Utilization of Geothermal Energy. *Science Communication*, 35 (6), 810–18.

Gross, M., 2014. The Social-ecological Co-constitution of Nature through Ecological Restoration: Experimentally Coping with Inevitable Ignorance and Surprise. *In*: Lockie, S., D. Sonnenfeld and D. Fisher, eds. *Routledge International Handbook of Social and Environmental Change*. London: Routledge, 269–79.

Gross, M. and Hoffmann-Riem, H., 2005. Ecological Restoration as a Real-World Experiment: Designing Robust Implementation Strategies in an Urban Environment. *Public Understanding of Science*, 14 (3), 269–84.

Gross, M. and Krohn, W., 2004. Science in a Real World Context: Constructing Knowledge through Recursive Learning. *Philosophy Today*, 48 (5), 38–50.

Gross, M. and McGoey, L., eds., 2015. *Routledge International Handbook of Ignorance Studies*. London: Routledge.

Grove-White R., 2001. New Wine, Old Bottles? Personal Reflections on the New Biotechnology Commissions. *The Political Quarterly*, 72 (4), 466–72.

Gupta, H. and Roy, S., 2007. *Geothermal Energy: An Alternative Resource for the 21st Century*. Amsterdam: Elsevier.

Haeckel, E., 1866. *Generelle Morphologie der Organismen. Allgemeine Grundzüge der organischen Formen-Wissenschaft, mechanisch begründet durch die von Charles Darwin reformirte Descendenz-Theorie (Vol. 2)*. Berlin, Germany: Reimer.

Haggett, C., 2011. Understanding Public Responses to Offshore Wind Power. *Energy Policy*, 39 (2), 503–10.

Heinberg, R., 2007. *Peak Everything: Waking Up to the Century of Declines*. Gabriola Island, BC: New Society Publishers.

Heinrichs, H., 2013. Dezentral und partizipativ? Möglichkeiten und Grenzen von Bürgerbeteiligung zur Umsetzung der Energiewende. *In*: Radke, J. and B. Hennig, eds. *Die deutsche 'Energiewende' nach Fukushima*. Marburg, Germany: Metropolis, 119–38.

Heiskanen, E. and Lovio, R., 2010. User–Producer Interaction in Housing Energy Innovations: Energy Innovation as a Communication Challenge. *Journal of Industrial Ecology*, 14 (1), 91–102.

Herbold, R., 1995. Technologies as Social Experiments: The Construction and Implementation of a High-Tech Waste Disposal. *In*: Rip, A.,

T. J. Misa, and J. Schot, eds. *Managing Technology in Society.* London: Pinter, 185–97.

Hess, D. J., 2012. *Good Green Jobs in a Global Economy: Making and Keeping New Industries in the United States.* Cambridge, MA: MIT Press.

Heymann, M., 1995. *Die Geschichte der Windenergienutzung, 1890–1990.* Frankfurt am Main: Campus Verlag.

Hoogma, R., Kemp, R., Schot, J. and Truffer, B., 2002. *Experimenting for Sustainable Transport: The Approach of Strategic Niche Management.* London: Spon Press/Taylor & Francis.

Horta, A., Wilhite, H., Schmidt, L. and Bartiaux, F., 2014. Socio-technical and Cultural Approaches to Energy Consumption: An Introduction. *Nature + Culture,* 9 (2), 115–21.

Howaldt, J., Kopp, R. and Schwarz, M., 2014. *Zur Theorie sozialer Innovationen: Tardes vernachlässigter Beitrag zur Entwicklung einer soziologischen Innovationstheorie.* Weinheim, Germany: Juventa.

Huang, S. and Liu, J., 2010. Geothermal Energy Stuck between a Rock and a Hot Place. *Nature,* 463, 293.

Huber, J., 2004. *New Technologies and Environmental Innovations.* Cheltenham, UK: Elgar.

Huenges, E., Kohl, T., Kolditz, O., Bremer, J., Scheck-Wenderoth, M. and Vienken, T., 2013. Geothermal Energy Systems: Research Perspective for Domestic Energy Provision. *Environmental Earth Sciences,* 70 (8), 3927–33.

Hughes, T. P., 1987. The Evolution of Large Technological Systems. *In:* Bijker, W. E., T. P. Hughes and T. J. Pinch, eds. *The Social Construction of Technological Systems.* Cambridge, MA: MIT Press, 51–82.

Humphrey, C. and Buttel, F. H., 1982. *Environment, Energy, and Society.* Belmont, CA: Wadsworth Publishing.

Huntington, E., 1924 [1915]. *Civilization and Climate.* New Haven, CT: Yale University Press.

Hyysalo, S., Juntunen, J. K. and Freeman, S., 2013. Internet Forums and the Rise of the Inventive Energy User. *Science & Technology Studies,* 26 (1), 25–51.

Ingram, M., 2012. Sculpting Solutions: Art–Science Collaborations in Sustainability. *Environment: Science and Policy for Sustainable Development,* 54 (4), 24–34.

Iskov, H. and Rasmussen, N. B., 2013. *Global Screening of Projects and Technologies for Power-to-gas and Bio-SNG. A Reference Report.* Hørsholm, Denmark: Danish Gas Technology Centre.

Jacobsson, S. and Lauber, V., 2006. The Politics and Policy of Energy System Transformation: Explaining the German Diffusion of Renewable Energy Technology. *Energy Policy*, 34 (3), 256–76.

Jepson, W., Brannstrom, C. and Persons, N., 2012. "We Don't Take the Pledge:" Environmentality and Environmental Skepticism at the Epicenter of US Wind Energy Development. *Geoforum*, 43 (4), 851–63.

Johnstone, N., 2005. The Innovation Effects of Environmental Policy Instruments. *In*: Horbach, J., ed. *Indicator Systems for Sustainable Innovation*. Heidelberg, Germany: Physica, 21–41.

Jorgenson, A. K., 2012. Energy: Analysing Fossil-fuel Displacement. *Nature Climate Change*, 2, 398–9.

Kagel, A. and Gawell, K., 2005. Promoting Geothermal Energy: Air Emissions Comparison and Externality Analysis. *Electricity Journal*, 18 (7), 90–9.

Karvonen, A. and van Heur, B., 2014. Urban Laboratories: Experiments in Reworking Cities. *International Journal of Urban and Regional Research* 38 (2), 379–92. DOI: 10.1111/1468-2427.12075.

Keirstead, J., 2007. Behavioural Responses to Photovoltaic Systems in the UK Domestic Sector. *Energy Policy*, 35 (8), 4128–41.

Kemp, R., Schot, J. and Hoogma, R., 1998. Regime Shifts to Sustainability through Processes of Niche Formation: The Approach of Strategic Niche Management. *Technology Analysis & Strategic Management*, 10 (2), 175–96.

Kerwin, A., 1993. None Too Solid: Medical Ignorance. *Knowledge: Creation, Diffusion, Utilization*, 15 (2), 166–85.

Kimberly, J. R., 1981. Managerial Innovation. *In*: Nystrom, P. C. and W. H. Starbuck, eds. *Handbook of Organizational Design: Volume 1*. Oxford, UK: Oxford University Press, 84–104.

Knies, G., Möller, U. and Straub, M., eds., 2008. *Clean Power from Deserts. The DESERTEC Concept for Energy, Water and Climate Security*. Bonn, Germany: Protext.

Kolditz, O., Jakobs, L. A., Huenges, E. and Kohl, T., 2013. Geothermal Energy: A Glimpse at the State of the Field and an Introduction to the Journal. *Geothermal Energy*, 1 (1), 1–2.

Kondratiev, N. D., 1926. Die langen Wellen der Konjunktur. *Archiv für Sozialwissenschaft und Sozialpolitik*, 56, 573–609.

König, A., ed., 2013. *Regenerative Sustainable Development of Universities and Cities: The Role of Living Laboratories*. Cheltenham, UK: Elgar.

Kousis, M., 1993. Collective Resistance and Sustainable Development in Rural Greece: The Case of Geothermal Energy on the Island of Milos. *Sociologia Ruralis*, 33 (1), 3–24.

Kowol, U. and Küppers, G., 2005. Innovation Networks: A New Approach to Innovation Dynamics. *In*: Geenhuizen, M., D. Gibson and M. Heitor, eds. *Regional Development and Conditions for Innovation in the Network Society*. West Lafayette, IN: Purdue University Press, 61–86.

Krauss, W., 2010. The 'Dingpolitik' of Wind Energy in Northern German Landscapes: An Ethnographic Case Study. *Landscape Research*, 35 (2), 195–208.

Kricher, J., 2009. *Balance of Nature: Ecology's Enduring Myth*. Princeton, NJ: Princeton University Press.

Krohn, W., 2007. Nature, Technology, and the Acknowledgment of Waste. *Nature + Culture*, 2 (2), 139–160.

Krohn, W. and Weingart, P., 1987. Nuclear Power as a Social Experiment: European Political 'Fall Out' From the Chernobyl Meltdown. *Science, Technology & Human Values*, 12 (2), 52–8.

Kunze, C., 2013. Die Energiewende und ihre geographische Diffusion. *In*: Gailing, L. and M. Leibenath, eds. *Neue Energielandschaften: Neue Perspektiven der Landschaftsforschung*. Wiesbaden, Germany: Springer-VS, 33–43.

Ladle, R. J. and Gillson, L., 2009. The (Im)Balance of Nature: A Public Perception Time-lag? *Public Understanding of Science*, 18 (2), 229–42.

Laird, F. N., 2013. Against Transitions? Uncovering Conflicts in Changing Energy Systems. *Science as Culture*, 22 (2), 149–56.

Latour, B., 1987. *Science in Action: How to Follow Scientists and Engineers through Society*. Cambridge, MA: Harvard University Press.

Laville, J. L. and Nyssens, M., 2001. The Social Enterprise: Towards a Theoretical Socio-economic Approach. *In*: Borzaga, C. and J. Defourny, eds. *The Emergence of Social Enterprise*. London: Routledge, 312–32.

Lehmann, P., 2013. Supplementing an Emissions Tax by a Feed-in Tariff for Renewable Electricity to Address Learning Spillovers. *Energy Policy*, 61, 635–41.

Lesser, W., 1987. *The Life below the Ground: A Study of the Subterranean in Literature and History*. Boston, MA: Faber & Faber.

Lönker, O., 2005. Ausgeträumt. *Neue Energie*, 6, 12.

MacDonald, D. W., 2011. Beyond the Group: The Implications of Roderick D. McKenzie's Human Ecology for Reconceptualizing Society and the Social. *Nature + Culture*, 6 (3), 263–84.

Manologlou, E., Tsartas, P. and Markou, A., 2004. Geothermal Energy Sources for Water Production: Socio-economic Effects and People's Wishes on Milos Island. *Energy Policy*, 32 (5), 623–33.

Markard, J. and Truffer, B., 2006. Innovation Processes in Large Technical Systems: Market Liberalization as a Driver for Radical Change? *Research Policy*, 35 (2), 609–25.

Martell, L., 1994. *Ecology and Society: An Introduction*. Cambridge, UK: Polity Press.

Mathews, J. A., 2013. Twelve Theses on the Greening of Capitalism: Is China Driving the Process? Paper presented at the Conference on *Financial Institutions for Innovation and Development*, Beijing, China, October 17–18.

Mautz, R., 2007. The Expansion of Renewable Energies in Germany between Niche Dynamics and System Integration: Opportunities and Restraints. *Science, Technology & Innovation Studies*, 3 (2), 113–31.

Mautz, R., 2012a. Atomausstieg und was dann? Probleme staatlicher Steuerung der Energiewende. *Der Moderne Staat: Zeitschrift für Public Policy, Recht und Management*, 5 (1), 149–68.

Mautz, R., 2012b. Sozioökonomische Dynamik der Energiewende. *In*: Forschungsverbund Sozioökonomische Berichterstattung, ed. *Berichterstattung zur sozioökonomischen Entwicklung in Deutschland. Teilhabe im Umbruch*. Wiesbaden, Germany: Springer-VS, 223–241.

Mautz, R. and Rosenbaum, W., 2012. Der deutsche Stromsektor im Spannungsfeld energiewirtschaftlicher Umbaumodelle. *WSI Mitteilungen*, 2, 85–93.

Mautz, R., Byzio, A. and Rosenbaum, W., 2008. *Auf dem Weg zur Energiewende. Die Entwicklung der Stromproduktion aus erneuerbaren Energien in Deutschland*. Göttingen, Germany: Universitätsverlag Göttingen.

Mayntz, R., 2009. *Über Governance: Institutionen und Prozesse politischer Regelung*. Frankfurt am Main, Germany: Campus Verlag.

Mazur, A. and Rosa, E., 1974. Energy and Life-style. *Science*, 186, 607–610.

McKenzie, R. D., 1926. The Scope of Human Ecology. *American Journal of Sociology*, 32 (1), 141–54.

McKinnon, A. M., 2010. Energy and Society: Herbert Spencer's 'Energetic Sociology' of Social Evolution and Beyond. *Journal of Classical Sociology*, 10 (4), 439–55.

Meyer, U. and Schubert, C., 2007. Integrating Path Dependency and Path Creation in a General Understanding of Path Constitution: The Role of Agency and Institutions in the Stabilisation of Technological Innovations. *Science, Technology & Innovation Studies*, 3 (1), 23–44.

Meyerhoff, J. and Petschow, U., 1999. Kurzschluss: Die Ausblendung ökologischer Folgekosten regenerativer Energien. *Politische Ökologie*, 61, 50–2.

Michael, M., 2012. When Things go Wrong. *In*: Seale, C., ed. *Researching Society and Culture*. London: Sage Publications, 543–54.

Miethling, B., 2011. Different but Similar: Geothermal Energy and the Role of Politics in Germany, Iceland and the United States. *Zeitschrift für Energiewirtschaft*, 35 (4), 287–96.

Milburn, C., 2012. Greener on the Other Side: Science Fiction and the Problem of Green Nanotechnology. *Configurations*, 20 (1–2), 53–87.

Mol, A. P. J., 2010. Social Theories of Environmental Reform: Towards a Third Generation. *In*: Gross, M. and H. Heinrichs, eds. *Environmental Sociology: European Perspectives and Interdisciplinary Challenges*. Dordrecht, Netherlands: Springer, 19–38.

Morris, C., 2012. Is Germany Switching to Coal? *In*: *Renewables International*, August 31. Available from: www.renewablesinternational.net (accessed June 17, 2013).

Mukuhira, Y., Asanuma, H., Niitsuma, H. and Häring, M. O., 2013. Characteristics of Large-magnitude Microseismic Events Recorded During and After Stimulation of a Geothermal Reservoir at Basel, Switzerland. *Geothermics*, 45 (1), 1–17.

Mumford, L., 1934. *Technics and Civilization*. New York, NY: Harcourt, Brace & Co.

Nadaï, A. and Labussière, O., 2010. Birds, Wind and the Making of Wind Power Landscapes in Aude, Southern France. *Landscape Research*, 35 (2), 209–33.

Nader, L., ed., 2010. *The Energy Reader*. Malden, MA: Wiley.

Nakajima, S., 2012. Prosumption in Art. *American Behavioral Scientist*, 56 (4), 550–69.

Nature, 2013. Editorial: Energy Crossroads. 496, 137–8.

Nordmann, A., 2009. European Experiments. *Osiris*, 24 (1), 278–302.

Nowotny H., Scott P. and Gibbons, M., 2001. *Rethinking Science: Knowledge and the Public in an Age of Uncertainty*. Cambridge, UK: Polity.

Ogburn, W. F., 1922. *Social Change: With Respect to Cultural and Original Nature*. New York, NY: Huebsch.

Ornetzeder, M. and Rohracher, H., 2006. User-led Innovations and Participation Processes: Lessons from Sustainable Energy Technologies. *Energy Policy*, 34 (2), 138–50.

Osti, G., 2014. Land Use Tensions for the Development of Renewable Sources of Energy. *In*: Lockie, S., D. Sonnenfeld and D. Fisher, eds. *Routledge International Handbook of Social and Environmental Change*. London: Routledge, 319–30.

Ostwald, W., 1909. *Energetische Grundlagen der Kulturwissenschaft*. Leipzig, Germany: Klinkhardt.

Ostwald, W., 1911. *Der energetische Imperativ*. Leipzig, Germany: Akademische Verlagsgesellschaft.

Packard, V., 1960. *The Waste Makers*. New York, NY: McKay.

Paech, N., 2013. Economic Growth and Sustainable Development. *In*: Angrick, M., A. Burger, and H. Lehmann, eds. *Factor X: Re-source – Designing the Recycling Society*. Dordrecht, Netherlands: Springer, 31–44.

Park, R. E. and Burgess, E. W., 1972 [1921]. *Introduction to the Science of Sociology*. Chicago, IL: University of Chicago Press.

Paschen, H., Oertel, D. and Grünwald, R., 2003. *Möglichkeiten geothermischer Stromerzeugung in Deutschland*. Berlin, Germany: Büro für Technikfolgen-Abschätzung beim Deutschen Bundestag (TAB).

Pasqualetti, M. J., 2011. Opposing Wind Energy Landscapes: A Search for Common Cause. *Annals of the Association of American Geographers*, 101 (4), 907–17.

Pasqualetti, M. J., Pick, J. B. and Butler, E. W., 1979. Geothermal Energy in Imperial County, California. *Energy*, 4 (1), 67–80.

Perlin, J., 1999. *From Space to Earth: The Story of Solar Electricity*. London: Earthscan.

Petroski, H., 2010. *The Essential Engineer: Why Science Alone Will Not Solve our Global Problems*. New York, NY: Vintage Books.

Petroski, H., 2012. *To Forgive Design: Understanding Failure*. Cambridge, MA: Harvard University Press.

Pinch, T. J. and Bijker, W. E., 1987. The Social Construction of Facts and Artifacts: Or How the Sociology of Science and the Sociology of

Technology Might Benefit Each Other. *In*: Bijker, W. E., T. P. Hughes, and T. J. Pinch, eds. *The Social Construction of Technological Systems*. Cambridge, MA: MIT Press, 17–50.

Podobnik, B., 1999. Toward a Sustainable Energy Regime: A Long-Wave Interpretation of Global Energy Shifts. *Technological Forecasting and Social Change*, 62, 155–72.

Podobnik, B., 2006. *Global Energy Shifts: Fostering Sustainability in a Turbulent Age*. Philadelphia, PA: Temple University Press.

Pohl, C. and Hirsch Hadorn, G., 2007. *Principles for Designing Transdisciplinary Research*. Munich, Germany: Oekom.

Praetorius, B., Bauknecht, D., Cames, M., Fischer, C., Pehnt, M., Schumacher, K. and Voß, J. -P., 2009. *Innovation for Sustainable Electricity Systems. Exploring the Dynamics of Energy Transitions*. Heidelberg, Germany: Physica.

Purkus, A. and Barth, V., 2011. Geothermal Power Production in Future Electricity Markets: A Scenario Analysis for Germany. *Energy Policy*, 39 (1), 349–57.

Pyka, A. and Küppers, G., eds., 2002. *Innovation Networks: Theory and Practice*. Cheltenham, UK: Elgar.

Rathmann, R., Szklo, A. and Schaeffe, R., 2010. Land Use Competition for Production of Food and Liquid Biofuels: An Analysis of the Arguments in the Current Debate. *Renewable Energy*, 35 (1), 14–22.

Rautio, P., 2011. Writing about Everyday Beauty: Anthropomorphizing and Distancing as Literary Practice. *Environmental Communication*, 5 (1), 104–23.

Raven, R., 2007. Niche Accumulation and Hybridization Strategies in Transition Processes towards a Sustainable Energy System: An Assessment of Differences and Pitfalls. *Energy Policy*, 35 (4), 2390–400.

Ravetz, J., 2012. The Significance of the Hamburg Workshop: Post-Normal Science and the Maturing of Science. *Nature + Culture*, 7 (2), 133–50.

Reich, M., 2009. *Auf Jagd im Untergrund: Mit Hightech auf der Suche nach Öl, Gas und Erdwärme*. Bad Salzdetfurth, Germany: AddBooks.

Reiche, D., 2002. Renewable Energies in the EU Member States in Comparison. *In*: Reiche, D., ed. *Handbook of Renewable Energies in the European Union. Case Studies of Member States*. Frankfurt am Main, Germany: Peter Lang, 13–24.

Reiche, D. and Bechberger, M., eds., 2006. *Ökologische Transformation der Energiewirtschaft: Erfolgsbedingungen und Restriktionen.* Berlin, Germany: Schmidt.

Rentzing, S., 2005. Drang auf die Dächer. *Neue Energie*, 7, 56–9.

Richards, E. S., 1907. *Sanitation in Daily Life.* Boston, MA: Whitcomb & Barrows.

Ritzer, G., Dean, P. and Jurgenson, N., 2012. The Coming of Age of the Prosumer. *American Behavioral Scientist*, 56 (4), 379–98.

Rogers, E. M., 1983. *Diffusion of Innovations.* New York, NY: Free Press.

Rohracher, H., 2008. Energy Systems in Transition: Contributions from Social Sciences. *International Journal of Environmental Technology and Management*, 9 (2–3), 144–61.

Rohrig, K., 2010. Interview with Kurt Rohrig (in German). *Technology Review*, April, 42–4.

Rosa, E., Machlis, G. E. and Keating, K. M., 1988. Energy and Society. *Annual Review of Sociology*, 14, 149–72.

Rosenbaum, W. and Mautz, R., 2011. Energie und Gesellschaft: Die soziale Dynamik der fossilen und der erneuerbaren Energien. *In:* Gross, M., ed. *Handbuch Umweltsoziologie.* Wiesbaden, Germany: Springer, 399–420.

Ross, E. A., 2009 [1901]. *Social Control: A Survey of the Foundations of Order.* New Brunswick, NJ: Transaction Publishers.

Rotmans, J. and Loorbach, D., 2010. Towards a Better Understanding of Transitions and Their Governance: A Systemic and Reflexive Approach. *In:* Grin, J., J. Rotmans and J. Schot, eds. *Transitions to Sustainable Development. New Directions in the Study of Long Term Transformative Change.* London: Routledge, 105–220.

Roy, B. N., 2002. *Fundamentals of Classical and Statistical Thermodynamics.* New York, NY: Wiley.

Rückert-John, J., ed., 2013. *Soziale Innovation und Nachhaltigkeit: Perspektiven sozialen Wandels.* Wiesbaden, Germany: Springer-VS.

Rybach, L., 2010. *Legal and Regulatory Environment Favorable for Geothermal Development Investors.* Paper presented at the World Geothermal Congress 2010, Bali, Indonesia, April 25–29, 2010. Available from www.geothermal-energy.org/pdf/IGAstandard/WGC/2010/0303.pdf (accessed March 1, 2014).

Sathyajith, M., 2006. *Wind Energy: Fundamentals, Resource Analysis and Economics.* Dordrecht, Netherlands: Springer.

Sauter, P., Witt, J., Billig, E. and Thrän, D., 2013. Impact of the Renewable Energy Sources Act in Germany on Electricity Produced with Solid Biofuels: Lessons Learned by Monitoring the Market Development. *Biomass and Bioenergy*, 53, 162–71.

Schäffle, A. F., 1878. *Bau und Leben des socialen Körpers* (2 vols.). Tübingen, Germany: Laupp.

Scheer, H., 2006. *Energy Autonomy: The Economic, Social and Technological Case for Renewable Energy*. London: Earthscan.

Scheer, H., 2012 [2010]. *The Energy Imperative: 100 Percent Renewable Now*. London: Earthscan.

Schilliger, P., 2011. *Geothermie – Die Alternative: Wie Erdwärme zu Elektrizität wird*. Altdorf, Switzerland: Gamm Druck & Verlag.

Schneider, L., 2012 [1975]. Ironic Perspective and Sociological Thought. *In*: Coser, L. A., ed. *The Idea of Social Structure: Papers in Honor of Robert K. Merton*. Piscataway, NJ: Transaction Publishers, 323–37.

Schneidewind, U. and Augenstein, K., 2012. Analyzing a Transition to a Sustainability-oriented Science System in Germany. *Environmental Innovation and Societal Transitions*, 3, 16–28.

Schot, J. and Geels, F. W., 2008. Strategic Niche Management and Sustainable Innovation Journeys: Theory, Findings, Research Agenda, and Policy. *Technology Analysis & Strategic Management*, 20 (5), 537–54.

Schreuer, A., 2013. The Rise of Citizen Power Plants in Germany. How do they emerge and spread? *Grassroots Innovations Research Briefing* 18, March 2013. Norwich and Brighton. Available from: www.grassrootsinnovations.org (accessed December 17, 2013).

Schreuer, A. and Weismeier-Sammer, D., 2010. *Energy Cooperatives and Local Ownership in the Field of Renewable Energy Technologies: A Literature Review*. Vienna: RICC – research report 2010/4.

Schulz, R., 2011. Energie aus der Tiefe: Geothermie. *In*: Renn, J., R. Schlögl and H. P. Zenner, eds. *Herausforderung Energie*. Berlin, Germany: Max Planck Research Library, 53–67.

Seyfang, G., 2009. *The New Economics of Sustainable Consumption*. Houndmills, UK: Palgrave Macmillan.

Seyfang, G., Park, J. J. and Smith, A., 2012. *Community Energy in the UK*. 3S Working Paper 2012–11. Norwich.

Shove, E., 2004. Sustainability, System Innovation and the Laundry. *In*: Elzen, B., F. W. Geels and K. Green, eds. *System Innovation and the Transition to Sustainability: Theory, Evidence and Policy*. Cheltenham, UK: Elgar, 76–94.

Sieferle, R. P., 1986. Die Laufenburger Stromschnellen: Eine Flussenge am Hochrhein erregt die Gemüter. *Bild der Wissenschaft*, 23 (7), 94–101.

Simmel, G., 1998 [1911]. *Philosophische Kultur: Gesammelte Essays*. Berlin, Germany: Wagenbach.

Slovic, P., 1987. Perception of Risk. *Science*, 236, 280–5.

Smil, V., 2010. *Energy Myths and Realities: Bringing Science to the Energy Policy Debate*. Lanham, MD: Rowman & Littlefield.

Smith, A., Voß, J. P. and Grin, J., 2010. Innovation Studies and Sustainability Transitions: The Allure of the Multi-level Perspective and its Challenges. *Research Policy*, 39 (4), 435–48.

Smithson, M., 1985. Toward a Social Theory of Ignorance. *Journal for the Theory of Social Behaviour*, 15 (2), 151–72.

Snyder, B. and Kaiser, M. J., 2009. A Comparison of Offshore Wind Power Development in Europe and the US: Patterns and Drivers of Development. *Applied Energy*, 86 (10), 1845–56.

Sohmer, M., 2012. *Untersuchungen zur Anwendbarkeit des Phased Array Prinzips für die seismische Vorauserkundung in gerichteten Tiefbohrungen*. Technical University of Freiberg, Germany: Dissertation at the Department of Geosciences, Geotechnology, and Mining.

Spencer, H., 1896 [1876]. *The Principles of Sociology* (3 vols.). London: Harrison and Sons.

Spreng, D., Flüeler, T., Goldblatt, D. L. and Minsch, J., eds., 2012. *Tackling Long-Term Global Energy Problems: The Contribution of Social Science*. Dordrecht, Netherlands: Springer.

SRU (Sachverständigenrat für Umweltfragen), ed., 2009. *Setting the Course for a Sustainable Electricity System. Five Propositions*. Berlin. Available from: www.umweltrat.de (accessed March 1, 2014).

Stern, P. C., Dietz, T. and Guagnano, G. A., 1995. The New Ecological Paradigm in Social-Psychological Context. *Environment and Behavior*, 27 (6), 723–43.

Sterner, M. and Jentsch, M., 2011. *Energiewirtschaftliche und ökologische Bewertung eines Windgas-Angebotes*. Gutachten für Greenpeace Energy. Kassel, Germany: Fraunhofer. Available from: www.greenpeace-energy.de/windgas/windgas-idee-mit-zukunft.html (accessed March 1, 2014).

Stirling, A., 2010. Keep it Complex. *Nature*, 468, 1029–31.

Strauss, S., Rupp, S. and Love, T., eds., 2013. *Cultures of Energy: Power, Practices, Technologies*. Walnut Creek, CA: Left Coast Press.

Sveiby, K. -E., Gripenberg, P. and Segercrantz, B., eds., 2012. *Challenging the Innovation Paradigm*. London: Routledge.

Szarka, N., Scholwin, F., Trommler, M., Jacobi, H. F., Eichhorn, M., Ortwein, A. and Thrän, D., 2013. A Novel Role for Bioenergy: A Flexible, Demand-oriented Power Supply. *Energy*, 61 (1), 18–26.

Teske, S., Pregger, T., Simon, S., Naegler, T., Graus, W. and Lins, C., 2011. Energy [R]evolution: A Sustainable World Energy Outlook. *Energy Efficiency*, 4 (3), 409–33.

Tushman, M. L. and Rosenkopf, L., 1992. Organizational Determinants of Technological Change. Toward a Sociology of Technological Evolution. *Research in Organizational Behavior*, 14, 311–47.

UBA (Umweltbundesamt), ed., 2013. *Daten zur Umwelt: Aktuelle Daten, Trends und Bewertungen zur Umweltsituation in Deutschland*. Dessau-Roßlau, Germany: UBA Publications.

Ulleberg, Ø., Nakken, T. and Eté, A., 2010. The Wind/Hydro Demonstration System at Utsira in Norway: Evaluation of System Performance using operational data and updated hydrogen energy system modeling tools. *International Journal of Hydrogen Energy*, 35 (5), 1841–52.

Urry, J., 2003. *Global Complexity*. Malden, MA: Blackwell.

Urry, J., 2013. *Societies beyond Oil: Oil Dregs and Social Futures*. London: Zed.

Vagiona, D. G. and Karanikolas, N. M., 2012. A Multicriteria Approach to Evaluate Offshore Wind Farms Siting in Greece. *Global Nest Journal*, 14 (2), 235–43.

van der Heijden, H. A., 2010. *Social Movements, Public Spheres and the European Politics of the Environment*. Houndmills, UK: Palgrave Macmillan.

van der Loo, F. and Loorbach, D., 2012. The Dutch Energy Transition Project, 2000–2009. *In*: Verbong, G. and D. Loorbach, eds. 2012. *Governing the Energy Transition: Reality, Illusion or Necessity?*. London: Routledge, 220–50.

Vasi, I. B., 2010. *Winds of Change: The Environmental Movement and the Global Development of the Wind Energy Industry*. Oxford, UK: Oxford University Press.

Verbong, G. and Geels, F. W., 2007. The Ongoing Energy Transition: Lessons from a Socio-technical, Multi-level Analysis of the Dutch Electricity System (1960–2004), *Energy Policy*, 35 (2), 1025–37.

Verbong, G. and Loorbach, D., eds., 2012. *Governing the Energy Transition: Reality, Illusion or Necessity?* London: Routledge.

Verne, J., 1992 [1864]. *Journey to the Center of the Earth*. Oxford, UK: Oxford University Press.

Vienken, T., Schelenz, S., Firmbach, L. and Dietrich, P., 2013. Development of Exploration and Monitoring Strategies for the Sustainable Thermal Use of the Shallow Subsurface. Paper presented at the Conference on *Novel Methods for Subsurface Characterization and Monitoring* (NovCare), Leipzig, Germany, May 13–16.

Walker, G., 2008. What are the Barriers and Incentives for Community-owned Means of Energy Production and Use? *Energy Policy*, 36 (12), 4401–5.

Weber, M., 1909. Energetische Kulturtheorien. *Archiv für Sozialwissenschaft und Sozialpolitik*, 29, 575–98.

Weber, M., 1978 [1920]. *Economy and Society: An Outline of Interpretive Sociology* (2 vols.). Berkeley, CA: University of California Press.

Weber, M., 2001 [1904]. *The Protestant Ethic and the Spirit of Capitalism*. London: Routledge.

Weber, M., 2003 [1923]. *General Economic History*. Mineaola, NY: Dover.

Wehrmann, A. K., 2013. Schlechtwetterlage auf dem Meer. *Neue Energie*, 6, 68–9.

Weinhold, N., 2006. Suche nach Erkenntnis. *Neue Energie*, 9, 25–31.

Werle, R., 2012. Institutions and Systems: Analysing Technical Innovation Processes from an Institutional Perspective. *In*: Bauer, J., A. Lang and V. Schneider, eds. *Innovation Policy and Governance in High-Tech Industries*. Heidelberg: Springer, 23–47.

Werner, R., 2007. Neue Netze für Europa. *Spiegel Special*, 1, 120–121.

West, P. C., 1985. Max Weber's Human Ecology of Historical Societies. *In*: Murvar, V., ed. *Theory of Liberty, Legitimacy and Power*. London: Routledge & Kegan Paul, 216–234.

Weyer, J., 2008. *Techniksoziologie: Genese, Gestaltung und Steuerung sozio-technischer Systeme*. Weinheim, Germany: Juventa.

White, L., 1949. *The Science of Culture: A Study of Man and Civilization*. New York, NY: Farrar, Straus & Giroux.

Wilhite, H., 2014. Sustainability as Social Practice: New Perspectives on the Theory and Policies of Reducing Energy Consumption. *In*: Lockie, S., D. Sonnenfeld and D. Fisher, eds. *Routledge International Handbook of Social and Environmental Change*. London: Routledge, 133–41.

Windeler, A., 2003. Kreation technologischer Pfade: ein strukturation-stheoretischer Analyseansatz. *In*: Schreyögg, G. and J. Sydow, eds. *Strategische Prozesse und Pfade*. Wiesbaden, Germany: Gabler, 295–328.

Winner, L., 1977. *Autonomous Technology: Technics-out-of-Control as a Theme in Political Thought*. Cambridge, MA: MIT Press.

Wolfe, P., 2008. The Implications of an Increasingly Decentralised Energy System. *Energy Policy*, 36 (12), 4509–13.

Woodman, B. and Baker, P., 2008. Regulatory Frameworks for Decentralised Energy. *Energy Policy*, 36 (12), 4527–31.

Wuppertal Institute/Centre de Recherche en Economie Appliquée pour le Développement (CREAD), 2010. *Algeria: A Future Supplier of Electricity from Renewable Energies for Europe?* Wuppertal, Germany: Heinrich Böll Foundation.

Wynne, B., 2005. Reflexing Complexity: Post-Genomic Knowledge and Reductionist Returns in Public Science. *Theory, Culture & Society*, 22 (5), 67–94.

York, R., 2012. Do Alternative Energy Sources Displace Fossil Fuels? *Nature Climate Change*, 2, 441–3.

INDEX

Made in the USA
Columbia, SC
25 October 2020